Richard Hammond was born in Birmingham in 1969. After Solihull School he studied photography and television production at art college. He worked for various radio stations including York, Cumbria, Newcastle, Lancashire and Leeds before moving to television. After stints on Sky's *Men and Motors*, *Motor Week* and *Better Cars*, he joined the BBC *Top Gear* team in 2002. His other television work includes presenting four series of *Brainiac: Science Abuse* for Sky One; *Petrolheads*, as a team captain, and *Time Commanders* for BBC2, and he was the host of *Richard Hammond's 5 O'Clock Show* for ITV1. He also presented *The Gunpowder Plot: Exploding the Legend*, *Should I Worry About* and *Richard Hammond and the Holy Grail* for BBC1, and Crufts Dog Show in 2005. He writes a weekly column for the *Daily Mirror*.

On 20 September 2006, he was critically injured in a car crash while filming for *Top Gear* at an airfield near York. He made a remarkable recovery and still lives in Gloucestershire with his wife Mindy and their two daughters, Izzy and Willow, four horses, five dogs, three cats, a duck called Slim, several motorcycles, a very old tractor and a large collection of cars.

Mindy Hammond was born in Cheltenham and, when she wasn't doing paper rounds to pay for her riding lessons, she went to the High School for Girls, Gloucester. Moving to London she worked in various offices, which paid for more riding lessons and fed the two big dogs with which she shared her small London flat. At night she wrote novels (still unpublished) and exercised too much. She met Richard in 1995 and together they moved to her home town, where she worked in graduate training. Following the birth of their two daughters she now divides her time between them, a menagerie of pets and livestock and managing Richard's increasing workload.

ON THE EDGE: MY STORY

RICHARD HAMMOND

With Mindy Hammond

PHOENIX

First published in Great Britain in 2007
by Orion
This abridged paperback edition published in 2008
by Orion Books Ltd, Orion House, 5 Upper Saint Martin's Lane
London WC2H 9EA

An Hachette Livre UK company

10 9 8 7 6 5 4 3

A CIP catalogue record for this book
is available from the British Library.

ISBN 978-0-7538-2330-9

Typeset by Input Data Services Ltd, Bridgwater, Somerset

Printed in Great Britain by Clays Ltd, St Ives plc

The Orion Publishing Group's policy is to use papers that
are natural, renewable and recyclable products and made
from wood grown in sustainable forests. The logging and
manufacturing processes are expected to conform to the
environmental regulations of the country of origin.

www.orionbooks.co.uk

CONTENTS

For Izzy & Willow

. . . and everyone who has suffered brain injury in any form, with best wishes and hope for the future

PREFACE

It's difficult for me to think of writing an introduction to my book for younger readers, because as far as I'm concerned I still am one. Let's be honest, most of what we do on *Top Gear* – and of what I do specifically – springs straight from our childish imaginations. And that's a good thing. The fact that our audience includes so many younger viewers tells me that we are doing it right. A lot of this book deals with the things I got up to as a lad – the bike jumps, the stunts, the falls – these are the formative events that turned me into whoever it is I am now.

So thank you, younger readers. I guess we're not so far apart in attitude, you and I, and it's good to know that you're interested. I hope you enjoy *On the Edge*. It's the story of what happens to a family when one member of it hangs very near the edge of this life and, eventually, comes back. And it's the story of what made me prepared to strap myself to the front of a jet engine with the power of 11 Formula One cars. Don't try it at home, is all I can say about that . . .

Chapter 1

PREPARING FOR
THE NORTH POLE

Instinct told me that I was watching one of those things that looked very easy to do but that would, in reality, turn out to be very difficult. My instructor glided across the flat, frozen fields in an effortless sweep, her long, thin skis moving in a languid rhythm, until she seemed to ripple over the snow in a single movement. She was demonstrating the classic cross-country-skiing style of her homeland and it looked as though she had spent her whole life doing it.

I knew that my efforts wouldn't look so good. And they didn't; I fell over, of course. I was discovering that cross-country skiing isn't just hard to perfect, it's almost impossible to get started.

It's mostly about grip, and I couldn't find any. And it's about rhythm (I didn't have any), poise (absolutely none) and grace (not a jot). Annoyingly, my first attempts didn't even amount to a hilarious high-speed crash. I just slithered about for a few seconds, my skis slipping backwards and forwards as I tried to waddle ahead before gravity won and I flopped on to my side and lay there, my nose inches from the frozen ground. But I wasn't learning this just for fun. In three months I would set off to the Magnetic North Pole on these same skis. Yet I couldn't cross a frozen playing field – and this was my third day of trying. I closed my eyes.

It got frightening inside my mind and panic rose in my chest. I was struggling because of the brain-damage. It must be that. I'd always been good at things when I tried them for the first time. A fast learner with a short attention span – pretty much every school report I ever had said exactly that. I had a vivid memory of my first attempt at water-skiing, behind a boat on Lake Windermere in the Lake District. I had listened half-heartedly while the bloke droned on about the need to keep your knees together, the need to keep the rope tight, and a thousand other things that I had to know. Eventually I slipped into the freezing grey waters and grabbed the plastic handle at the end of the blue nylon rope. The boat started to pull away and then there was a gentle but firm tug on the rope as the small boat reached the limit of the line. I gripped hard, there was a lot of splashing, I gripped some more and eventually rose up from the foam like a small, straggly Neptune in a borrowed blue wetsuit. I was water-skiing; it was easy. I got cocky and waved at a boat going the other way. Logic told me that I could shift my weight across the skis to change direction, and it worked. Crossing the wake, one of my skis was pulled off by the turbulent water. I shifted over to my right leg and carried on.

My wife, Mindy, can still hardly bear to talk about our first horse-riding trips together. She has been riding all her life. Usual sort of thing: spent half her childhood being shouted at by stern-faced women about her leg position and posture in the saddle. Horse-riding is, for her, an art. She approaches it with the same respect, consideration and, yes, fear that a test pilot might approach each flight. By contrast,

I wandered up to the first nag, hopped on board, asked how you steered and braked it, and set off. There was no need to shout at me about leading legs or how I held the reins. I still ride horses in the same way as I did that first time: I get on, pull left to go left and right to go right, and make sure I don't fall off. It drives Mindy mad. I have always been like this; I love trying anything new and can usually make a decent go of it the first time I try it. If I have to learn how to do it properly, I get bored and want to do something I know I'm already good at.

Lying on the snowy ground, I became convinced that my inability to just leap on to the skis and dazzle my instructor must be down to the aftermath of the jet-car crash. On the way there, I had harboured a secret suspicion that she might watch my first tries at mastering the finer points of the classic Swedish cross-country-skiing style and suggest that I try a competition or two, just for fun. I might even have the makings of an international cross-country skier – if there are such things. Right now, she was more likely to suggest I took up collecting Alpine horns, or yodelling.

It might have been funny, but I knew that I was only struggling with this because I had damaged something important in my brain that would never fix. I must have dented my balancing gland or disconnected my coordination centre. Or something. Whatever it was, I wished I hadn't done it.

The wet snow started to penetrate the damp fleece I had been issued by the polar experts who had brought us here for our pre-expedition training. The rest of the guys were flying back that morning; they'd no need to learn to ski: they were going to the Pole in a truck. Which meant right now, on this cold and lonely Austrian morning, they could go home. I thought of Mindy, the kids, the dogs and our house. And I thought of that sodding crash and the pain it had caused.

Chapter 2

THE EARLY YEARS OF AN ADRENALIN JUNKIE

I waited and silently weighed up the chances of actually becoming airborne. If the stunt went wrong and I hit the ramp too fast, there was a real chance that I might take off. I tightened my grip on the handlebars and swallowed hard. The crowd was a big one. I had better not look scared. I shook my head in what I hoped was a heroic, preparing-yourself-to-do-something-really-dangerous sort of way. I didn't know it, or want to know it, but all the rest of the world could see was a spindly-legged eight-year-old sitting on a red bicycle.

The bike looked brilliant, I knew that for a fact. I had tied two school satchels to the back and draped them over the rack to hang down on either side like motorcycle panniers. There was a fresh piece of cardboard in place, ripped from an old Weetabix packet and fixed to the chainstay with a strip of electrical tape I had found stuck to the garage floor. When I set off for the ramp, the cardboard would rattle away in the spokes and I would sound exactly like a California Highway Patrol bike giving chase to a fleeing villain on the telly. At least in my eight-year-old imagination I would. I hoped I would to the assembled gang of neighbourhood kids watching now, all secretly hoping my attempt to leap into the history books would produce blood and possibly a sighting of actual bone protruding through flesh, like that kid in the year above was rumoured to have done the previous year when he fell off a fence and broke his arm on an upended patio slab.

We often spoke about that, hunched in groups among the dustbins between the semis on our road. We loved talking about gore. And we loved our bikes. I once leaned mine in the narrow gap between the two walls and used it as a booster step to set me on my way, climbing up, braced between our garage wall and the side of the house next door. I began shuffling upwards, feeling the rough texture of the red bricks, surprisingly warm on my palms, hearing the nylon rasp of my jacket catching on the brickwork and scrabbling for traction with my trainers. The next thing I knew, my bike had collapsed to the floor and I slid down the wall to join it in a tangled pile of wheels, legs and framework. It didn't really hurt, and it looked great. Loads of my friends saw it and I started a new craze for wall climbing in the alleyways between our houses. Result for me.

Years later, I would be in at the start of a similar craze at school. We discovered that you could, just, make the climb from one balcony across to another in the big school hall where we would sit for assembly and the clever kids would gather for classical music recitals during lunch breaks. As they sawed at their violins, I would totter above them, stepping out from the curtains that flanked what amounted to a sort of theatre box and feeling for the edge of the next box with my foot. When I felt the time was right I would throw my weight across to the extended leg and find myself standing on the edge of the neighbouring balcony. Boy, did that one catch on.

My regular stunt activities were a survival technique I had evolved. If you're a small guy and can't impose yourself on others physically, then think of something funny to say. When you run out of funny things to say, hit yourself in the face with a bicycle pump. Goes down a storm every time.

Comedy is a great way of making up for other shortcomings in your life; ask any comedian. Hurting yourself for the amusement of others is even better. I learned my lesson pretty early on and now, at the age of eight, I was a master of the pratfall, the comedy trip and the pretend faint. It probably helped that I was small and light; when I dropped out of a tree, fell off a bike or walked into a lamp-post, there wasn't the kinetic energy generated by one of the big kids doing the same thing. When they fell, they broke bones. When I fell, I just bounced, laughed and checked that someone was watching.

I would spend hours trying to impress the girl next door. She would sit on her swing, bored, while I looned about on the other side of the fence, telling jokes, making up stories and reciting lines from favourite cartoons. When I eventually ran out of jokes, I would resort to just throwing myself about in an attempt to fly, or leap clear over the flower-beds. It worked every time. A few falls, a slip on the crazy paving, a dive into the shrubbery and she would be riveted like a Bond girl watching her fella shin up a cliff and take out a legion of baddies armed with nothing but a bottle opener and his razor-sharp wit.

Other kids hung around after school and built models out of giant milk straws to try to impress the teachers; the really bad kids set fire to trees in the playing fields or broke into school buildings. I set up ramps and tried to jump over stuff on bikes, attempted clearly impossible leaps across giant chasms, and climbed trees until I felt sure the air got thinner.

My first love was my bike. I've always loved whatever

two-wheeled transport I've owned. I still do today, though now, of course, it has an engine. I sat down with my father when I was eight and worked out just how many days there were until I could drive a car. When I discovered that there were 365 days fewer to wait before I could ride a bike, doing so became an all-consuming passion I would never lose. The walls of the bedroom I shared with my two brothers, Nick and Andy, were decorated with Chopper bikes that I stared at until I fell asleep. Stunt legend and motorcycling hero Evel Knievel was my idol, even though I had never really seen him in action (this was before sports channels on satellite TV put every loony in the limelight for all to admire or laugh at). I may never have seen him do it, but I knew what he did, and I adored him for it. It was the combination of showmanship, theatre and downright lunatic bravery that set my imagination on fire.

The bike I sat on now, secretly scared as the crowd grew impatient for the action to begin, was a small red bicycle styled to look like a racing bike, but sadly it didn't carry the look through into the technical department. The wheels were fairly narrow, but also small in diameter, so they never looked like the sleek skinny ones on the real racers. I was proud of the glamorous yellow racing tape coiled around the dropped handlebars and fixed in place at the ends by blue plastic plugs, but the plugs were forever coming unstuck. But perhaps the most pressing concern I had was the lack of gears. It looked like a racer, albeit a small one, but gears were the defining element of such things. Mine had none. Not a single gear. It was a fixed speed with a single cog at the back and not a hope of changing it. I used to ride everywhere at top speed, not to get there quicker but in the hope that anyone who didn't already know would not clock that my otherwise glamorous and good-looking steed had no gears.

That didn't stop me loving it though. It was still the best, the most perfect, the handsomest and, of course, the fastest bike in the whole world. My parents bought it second-hand from the huge bicycle shop near Robin Hood Island on the outskirts of Birmingham. It was the most exciting purchase I had ever been involved in, and the arrival of any new car or motorbike in my life since has struggled to eclipse that moment.

Right now, my pride and joy felt heavy, unsteady and infinitely precious. I didn't want to hit the deck hard and scuff it – or me – if things went wrong. Way ahead in the distance – probably twenty or thirty feet – waited the ramp. We had made it from a piece of thin shiny wood, probably a melamine cast-off from someone's kitchen. A couple of house bricks pilfered from the pile at the side of our shed held it up. Beyond that was the pile of clobber I'd have to clear. And there was a crowd of people waiting for me to do it.

The ragtag band of kids from our suburban street in Shirley, West Midlands, had started that Saturday afternoon in the usual way, tearing around on bicycles, arguing over toy cars and spraying each other with machine-gun fire from behind the low-lying brick walls that surrounded our homes. When we'd grown bored, I had suggested we set up the jump. Along the way, I may have made a boast or two about how good I was at jumping over things, so we'd ended up with the ramp. The goal started out as being to clear my mate's Action Man, lying prostrate at the end of the ramp in his Desert Combat kit. Another Action Man was added, then another. Of course, I decided that that wasn't enough; the jump had to be bigger, the spectacle more stomach-churning. We added a plastic helicopter with guns on it that fired little pellets of paper when you flicked a spring backwards with a plastic tag on the side, and the fabulous wooden Jeep my grandfather had built for Action Man to tear around imaginary war zones in. It would take a big jump to clear the resulting heap.

The confidence I had felt earlier faded as I sat summoning up the courage to go through with the plan. The preparations had taken a long time and the spectators' interest was rapidly cooling. A scuffle broke out. I was losing their attention. I tried not to cry.

Then I decided to take the plunge and risk physical pain. Needless to say, it was pathetic. I got a bit of a wobble on midway through the run-up to the ramp. Correcting the wobble used up precious momentum, and the ramp itself was too bendy to hold the weight of the bike. It bowed to touch the pavement beneath as the front wheel rolled on to it. The leading edge of the ramp, supported on two bricks, couldn't bend so stood proud immediately in front of my back wheel. It hit, I stopped quickly, and flopped over the side and on to the ground. It wasn't an exciting fall: there was no damage to the bike, Action Man's head stayed on, the helicopter and the Jeep made it through to fight another day, there was no blood from me and no chance of a glimpse of real bone through ripped flesh, like that kid in the year above. By the time we had hidden the bricks, slotted the piece of plastic wood down the side of a neighbour's garage and checked my knees for scabs, the event was forgotten and we had moved on to talking about the kid from the year above who fell and chopped off both his arms and his head on an upended patio slab.

The big plus about an early life spent performing low-rent stunts is that you quickly find it is possible to get by with absolutely no skills whatsoever. You don't have to be good at anything in order to hurt yourself for the amusement of others; in fact, it helps if you're not. I was a daredevil, sure, but all that meant when I was a kid was that I was prepared to fall over and didn't mind too much when I grazed the odd knee or elbow. There was little point in spending hours practising keepie-uppie with a football or solving a Rubik's Cube in under two minutes if you could earn more admiration by leaping over a ditch full of imaginary alligators on to a bank full of very real stinging nettles. I took the leap, every time. So you would think that when new, exciting and seemingly dangerous crazes came along, I was among the first to welcome them with open arms. But no, I never really welcomed the change.

My world revolved around my pedal cars when I was younger and, eventually, my bike. When skateboards became the rage my friends were all to be found slithering around the streets, practising jumps, turns, and that really annoying manoeuvre where they leap in the air and flip the board underneath their feet before landing on it again. I just rode my bike up and down the street and fell off into a hedge every now and then in the hope that someone was watching. Only once did I borrow a neighbour's skateboard. After a brief blast up and down the pavement outside our front garden, I decided it wasn't for me and got back on my bike. As soon as I learned to wobble up and down the pavement standing on the board, I got an inkling of just how long it would take to learn how to do stunts on it, decided it was too long and gave up. I haven't been on a skateboard since.

Then BMX bikes arrived. Everyone around me, even adults, hurtled about on their brightly coloured little bikes and thought they were cool. I never had one. I didn't want one. While my friends practised their flips and turns on a home-made half-pipe, I hurtled about on a racing bike – one with ten gears by then – and got my kicks from going fast. There was always some muppet leaping about as a guest on *Blue Peter* and showing us how clever he was by riding his BMX while sitting on the handlebars, or standing on the seat. I was happy enough hurtling down the hill between my house and the paper shop where I picked up my round, and seeing if I could keep up with cars.

But there was one area where I could be persuaded to apply myself. I didn't just love bikes for what they could do; I loved them for how they worked. I was fascinated by the mechanical processes going on and could, even as an eight-year-old, rebuild one pretty much with my eyes shut. By the time I was ten or eleven I was confident enough to strip them down to the last nut and bolt and restore them to smooth-running perfection. In fact, I was never happier than when I was up to my neck in piles of cotter-pins, bearings, brake blocks and chainsets. I spent several weeks rebuilding my brother Andy's racer for him. It was a metallic red Peugeot and had been in need of a little attention. Andy was, I think, more interested in the bike as a means of transport, but he was happy enough for me to take it off the road and mess about with it. I was overjoyed at having another project to get stuck into, particularly one that involved fiddling about with someone else's bike, leaving mine intact for getting to school and showing off afterwards.

The work was done mostly on the area of patio immediately outside the garden shed. Sitting on the paving slabs, I would wrestle with stubborn bolts, often gouging holes in my palms with the sharp-edged multi-spanner and plastic-handled screwdriver that made up my tool kit. If heavy-duty weapons were needed, Dad was happy to let me raid his big metal toolbox inside the shed, as long as I put stuff back. Which I invariably failed to do.

After what seemed like months of work, the job was done. It was magnificent; a gleaming array of smooth-running, well-oiled efficiency. Every moving part had been removed, fiddled with, lubricated and replaced. Andy was delighted, though I now suspect he may have been humouring me. It had to be test-ridden and that, categorically, was a job for me. Test-riding was, of course, the best bit about being a bike mechanic.

You learn a lot on the test ride, and not just about the bicycle you are testing, but about physics and life in general. I once fitted Chopper handlebars to a racing bike and test-rode it down the hill. When I dabbed the front brake, my weight was transferred to the handlebars. Because the Chopper bars were longer than the standard dropped ones, my weight was transferred to a point much further from the headstock of the bike. This, effectively, increased the leverage exerted on the headstock under braking; in this instance, it became the pivot. I learned a valuable lesson in levers and forces when I smashed my face into the headstock as the bars collapsed forward and failed to support me, throwing me off the saddle to mash my goolies into the crossbar as I hurtled towards the ground. The front wheel of the bike connected with a low wall; the wheel, together with the wall, then acted as yet another pivot, and the whole lot – me, the bike and my newly acquired appreciation for the basic principles of physics – crashed over the wall and into a bush. I had an opportunity to combine this science lesson with a horticultural one, for the bush had vicious one-inch spikes all over it. But I had lost interest in learning by then and wanted to cry instead.

I got myself ready to put Andy's bike through its paces.

Several houses down from ours was a side road. It split off from the main road and made its way round a triangular patch of grass surrounded by houses before rejoining our street further up. This was known among us kids as 'the Triangle'. Some would use it for exploring, some for playing chase. I used it for testing stuff. Residents along that stretch must have grown used to looking both ways twice as they left their front drives, because there was every likelihood that I might streak past at a scaled-down 200 mph while testing out a rebuilt bike, scooter or tea tray with wheels and string to steer it. That day, though, I was planning to break all records.

The bike was working beautifully and I shifted through the gears to check I had adjusted the cables correctly. The chainset ticked smoothly when I freewheeled, but mostly I just kept pouring in the power with my frantically twirling trainers. It being a triangle, there were three corners in the road. I powered down the main straight, rounded the first corner, which was a gentle bend, then hit the second straight, turned right and sped towards the last corner.

There was never much traffic on the Triangle, which was why we were allowed to play there. It also meant that it took a long time for the loose chippings left after recent works to be worn into the surface of the road. As I leaned the bike over to make the turn and shoved yet more power through the crank, I hit a deep patch of loose gravel. The front wheel started to slip away and that was it. I was into a crash. The first part of me to hit the deck was my right hand. I removed most of the skin on several fingers and a coin-shaped chunk of flesh from my right shoulder. In the hospital, they had to trim away the dead skin and tidy up the wounds. I swore blind you could see the white bone of my little finger's knuckle through the ripped and tortured flesh. It stung like hell when they painted it with iodine, but I couldn't wait to get back and show my mates at home. I had seen the bone.

Of course, when someone goes off the rails, even in a jet car like I did, it's all too easy to say 'blame the parents'. In fact, my mum and dad never encouraged the daredevil in me, but neither did they try to suppress it. With three sons to raise, they grew used to the fact that one of us would always have gravel rash on his knees, plasters on his elbows and a bruise on his face. It was usually me. They certainly never wrapped me in cotton wool. But they were dealing with the product of their genes, and therein lay the problem.

My father's father, my grandpa, George Hammond, was a tall, outwardly gentle man, possessing a gentle, soft-spoken nature that was utterly compelling. What I never appreciated, though, was that this calm, kind man was also capable of almost reckless bravery. While serving in the RAF during the Second World War he volunteered for bomb disposal duty. This meant sitting for hours down dark, damp holes or hastily improvised shafts, working on a bomb that could explode at any moment and kill you and your mates. While my father lay at home in Birmingham as a baby, Grandpa tinkered with German bombs. When the war ended, it must have been tricky for Grandpa to fill a considerable vacuum of excitement in his life. He seems to have come back to his family desperate for tranquillity and peace. But he did, occasionally, remind the world that danger was, for him, not something to be scared of. My father tells me now that not once did his father turn off the mains electricity when fixing a light switch or a plug socket. He would stand there, screwdriver held calmly in his hand, and carry out the task. Occasionally he would accidentally complete the circuit with his screwdriver and get the full force of the mains electricity through his body. On one such occasion he was thrown backwards through the glass roof of the conservatory; on another he toppled off the banister he was balancing on and fell down the stairs. His response was to swear softly, dust himself off and get back on with the job. This was not deliberate thrill-seeking, I am sure, but there must have been a love of adrenalin deep inside my gentle, caring grandpa. And I am equally sure that I inherited a strand of it.

From the other side of our family, from my mother's father, I inherited my passion for machines, engineering and, in particular, cars. Grandad had trained as a cabinet-maker and later worked as a coachbuilder, using wood to build the frames that held the hand-built aluminium car bodies together. He could carve wood, turn metal, work leather and improvise a way of making anything out of anything. The attic at the home he shared in Birmingham with my grandmother and great-grandmother was a place of magic for a six-year-old boy. Grandad would lead the way through workshops crammed with vices, lathes and other tools I didn't understand. Huge pillar drills glistened in dark corners and racks of cleaned-out jam jars and tobacco tins contained screws, bolts, washers and fittings of every size and nature. Nothing was wasted. When finally something was beyond even his help it would be stripped for parts, and those parts dropped into neatly labelled tins for use on another day. And that day always came. He could make everything: pedal cars, go-karts, sideboards, fancy-dress costumes, tables, cupboards and carvings emerged in a constant stream from his workshop. I stood in awe of his skill and engineering intelligence; it would be a proud thing indeed if today I could say I had inherited a fraction of it along with the passion for cars that I undoubtedly owe to him.

But the evidence is clear. From these gentlemen I inherited two things: a love of cars and engineering, and an almost equal passion for daredevilry and danger. So, please, let's not blame my parents. Let's blame their parents.

Chapter 3

FROM LOCAL RADIO TO *TOP GEAR*

Like any major road, the A40 into London has many landmarks along its length. Among them is a pale concrete footbridge extending over the four lanes of carriageway. Anyone queuing miserably along that stretch of road on the morning of 19 February 2002 searching the grey day for something to distract them might have made out a small figure in jeans and a leather jacket sloping across the bridge to stand and stare out over the damp and dreary wastelands stretching alongside the road. An idle commuter's mind might have constructed all manner of romantic motivations for this stranger's solitary amble. A lover spurned? A desperate man, contemplating something dreadful on this Wednesday morning? No, it was me, and I was crapping myself. At eleven o'clock I was due to audition for a job on the all-new *Top Gear* programme.

At the time, I was working for Granada as a presenter on car and bike shows on satellite TV, and this was my dream opportunity. I spent my time zipping around the country to film reviews of cars and bikes for shows that had smaller audiences than the film crew on most big-budget TV programmes. It may have been small, but it had been an excellent place to practise and I felt that now I was ready to move up. All I needed was the right opportunity – and this was it. It was like someone leaning over the fence as you played football with your mates to invite you to try out for Manchester United.

I had gone for a walk to steady my nerves, and to try to kill the half-hour or so before the audition. I stood at the top of the concrete stairs and gripped the cold metal handrail. My efforts to calm myself with deep breathing left me light-headed. I tried to convince myself that it was no big deal; I would either get the job or I wouldn't, and then I would go back home to Cheltenham and life would carry on as normal. Maybe it would be better if I just drove home now and didn't put myself through the misery of cocking it up. Maybe they had already made up their minds and I was wasting my time. This was not helping. Realising that standing there getting all miserable was hardly going to make me shine in the audition, I turned and walked snappily back over the bridge.

Looked at from the right angle, my life had been pretty much leading towards this moment. After a childhood dedicated almost entirely to fooling around in pedal cars and on bicycles and obsessing about cars and motorbikes, my adult life had seemed to plot a course for this point as inevitably as a well-steered ship heading for port. I went to art college in Harrogate and spent my time taking photographs of scrapyards and painting pictures of American muscle cars. My photos and paintings can't have been very good: I finished art college and went straight to work in the least visual of all media, radio.

My first job was as a reporter at BBC Radio North Yorkshire. For an eighteen-year-old lad, a career in broadcasting seemed almost impossibly exciting. Inside, the station boasted a sophisticated luxury beyond my wildest dreams. There was a full-time receptionist, a kitchen with a microwave where we could heat our own pasties, and a production office in which every horizontal surface supported stacks of papers and reel-to-reel tapes high enough to connect with the ceiling.

Best of all, there were the studios. On my first visit, I was taken to stand in awe at the back of studio 1A and look through the glass to the neighbouring studio. A terrifying On Air light glowed red overhead as the presenter slid faders, pushed buttons and turned dials, all the time talking smoothly into an enormous microphone suspended from a cradle of black elastic overhead. He laughed confidently, twisted a dial with his left hand, flicked a fader downwards and introduced another caller to the airwaves. I was mesmerised and swore that one day I would do that. In the meantime, there was coffee to be made for the production team upstairs.

I had a great deal to learn, and I spent the next ten years trying to learn it. Hopping from radio station to radio station, I lived in a series of bedsits and shared houses all over the north of England while honing my skills interviewing, editing, dodging news meetings and running away from angry farmers who didn't want to talk about subsidies for the evening news. I interviewed government ministers, authors, children's entertainers, celebrity chefs, adventurers and craftspeople. I spoke with people who had performed amazing feats, won incredible contests, battled terrible illness and started successful businesses. I learned that all of us, each and every one, lives a life that is, in its own right, an epic.

I did eventually host a live show from that studio at BBC Radio North Yorkshire. It was a lunchtime slot on the Sunday – traditionally, the training ground for new presenters. My housemate, Andy Breare, now an established broadcaster on radio and television, had already taken the plunge and presented his first show. He put in a fantastic performance in which he sounded like a seasoned presenter of a thousand shows, and afterwards made light of it in the station kitchen. I knew that I would be convulsed with fear when my turn came.

On the morning of my first show, I walked into the station almost blind with terror and sat in the production office trying to stop my hands from shaking. The show, *Last Week in North Yorkshire*, was a two-hour review of highlights from the week's broadcasting. In an hour's time I would be going it alone. It didn't do to dwell on the terror of what was to come, so I kept myself busy. I read the papers, hoping to find funny stories. There was nothing. I read and re-read the assortment of printed scripts and handwritten jottings that would form the introductions to the various clips I would be playing. I checked and rechecked the box full of tapes I had to play. The clock moved on. I limped downstairs to the studio, stopping off at the toilets on the way for what I can distinctly recall was the seventh visit of the morning. I made it to the desk, shook like a leaf and, when the time came, got started.

I still have a taped copy of the show. It wasn't brilliant. As the news ends and a station jingle is played, the tiny voice of a young man clearly scared half out of his wits does its best to rise above the dying chords. I introduce myself and mistime the introduction to Dusty Springfield's 'Son of a Preacher Man'. As my tremulous voice stomps all over the opening lyrics, my broadcasting career begins. There were more cock-ups as the show progressed. At one point I left the microphone open while answering the telephone to a caller during a record. As the music plays, I can be heard in the background until suddenly I go silent. I have noticed the mic fader is still open. You can almost hear me gulp. The record ends and I make a pathetic attempt to pretend I left it open on purpose by telling listeners, 'Well, that was the first caller, erm, you, erm, could be the next. Just call me on – oh, I've lost the number. Call me on the, er, the phone.'

Sitting in my car with a stomach full of butterflies some thirteen years later, I still cringe at the memory of it. The car is a 1982 Porsche 911 SC. The red paintwork is far from perfect, the headlining is green with mildew, the engine rattles ominously over three thousand revs, the rev counter doesn't count the revs, the oil gauge doesn't gauge the oil, and the huge teatray spoiler on the back reminds other drivers of stockbrokers in red braces and inspires them to gesticulate at me accordingly. It's the best car I have ever owned and I adore it.

On the day I collected it, I drove it over to my parents' house in Leatherhead. It was autumn but the rain had stopped briefly and I took in the lustrous red paintwork, admiring the way the raindrops formed round, silver pearls over the car's broad flanks. I twirled the key-fob in my fingers and hit the button to lock the doors – the first car I had ever owned with central locking. My mother and father sensed immediately that I was there on a showing-off mission and they 'oohed' and 'aahed' accordingly. This was a routine they had slipped into many times over the years: I would always turn up in whatever set of wheels I had ruined myself financially to own and they would always oblige by listening to my breathless demonstration of the car's finer points and my patient explanation of why this was the single best car ever produced by anyone, ever. They would even bite their tongues and endure my manic attempts to justify the expense of such a vehicle when I could hardly afford a new pair of jeans. How they did this, time after time, I just don't know. But I thank them for it, and for playing along with my daft game, from the bottom of my heart. Of course, the fact that my father can recall going through almost the exact same process in his younger years may well have helped a little.

Even when work was trickling along nicely, there was always a far-too-large chunk of my mind dwelling on cars and motorbikes. I spent most of my young adult life looking over the boss's shoulder at the car park beyond and dreaming which car I would go for if I had the choice and how I would set about improving it. It was that very car park, though, that nearly finished my radio career before it began. Turning up for my first day's work at Radio York in 1988, I found the car park filled with dreary hatchbacks, rusty Ford Escorts and assorted family cars. I had anticipated a car park resembling the pit lane at an exotic race-meet, packed full of Ferraris, Jaguars, Aston Martins and beautiful sporty classics. What I saw was a car park like you'd find outside any supermarket. This came as a sizeable disappointment and one that very nearly had me turning on my heel and looking for a job in big finance or gun-running. If I wasn't going to be able to afford at least a hot hatch, then did I really want to shackle myself to a life in the media?

But I soon found that there were small compensations to be had for the car fanatic working in radio. Whenever I reported for duty at yet another northern radio station – a common occurrence, thanks to the ebb and flow of life as a freelance – I would secretly nip down to the garage to check out the radio car. Every station had one, and using it was possibly the part of the job I liked best. It lived alone in a large garage, typically tended by a team of two or three sound engineers who jealously guarded the vehicle and the associated piles of cables and outdoor broadcast equipment. The car, or sometimes a van, would be equipped with a mast that could, at the flick of a switch, extend ten metres or so into the sky to allow the aerial on top to connect with base and establish a broadcasting link.

Every station had its legendary horror story concerning a rookie reporter who went out with the radio car to make a report. Inevitably, the reporter in the tale flicked the switch to send the mast up into power cables suspended from a pylon immediately overhead. Depending on the humour of the sound engineer telling you the story, it then became increasingly grisly, sometimes incorporating details such as the hapless reporter gripping the microphone ever tighter as the current increased until they resembled a fried snack stuck to the end of a melted boa constrictor. Needless to say, the important message was one concerning the need to check overhead for power lines before setting up the mast.

Once the mast was successfully erected and the wise operator not fried, he could then feed live reports into the station's output. I reported on farm animal breakouts, jumble sales and sponsored swims. But for me, the job peaked when I turned the key in the ignition and pulled out of the garage. They were not, generally, glamorous cars; BBC budgetary constraints that I did not understand at the time ruled out a radio-Lamborghini. But after a lifetime spent coaxing a few more miles out of whatever wheezy old banger I could afford, the opportunity to drive an almost brand-new car was too good to miss. Radio North Yorkshire had a fleet of brand-new Escorts for dashing out to record reports for the news bulletins. I would hover around the newsroom, hoping that the editor would call for someone to record an interview and, finding no proper report-ers available, would send me out instead. It only happened once, and it was to interview a bus driver within walking distance of the station.

On my first day at Radio Newcastle, they sent me out in the radio van to report from what I did not at the time realise was a famously rough estate. I found my way to the school I was due to report from and set up the mast. I unwound the drum of thick green cable, attached the microphone and headphones to the end, connected it to the van and threaded my way in across the playground and into the school hall. I introduced myself to the teacher and the kids, popped the headphones on and prepared to hit the ground running when the presenter gave me the cue. Through the headphones I heard him announce my name and the location, then I swung into action. As soon as I started speaking, the headphones went dead. I carried on regardless, interviewing staff and pupils, and signed off cheerily. When I went back out to the van, I discovered that I had left the door unlocked and the end of the cable had been torn out and the interior stripped and trashed. I didn't work there for very long.

While working at Radio Lancashire I experienced something of a revelation. I took over as producer and presenter of the weekend mid-morning shows, and I inherited a range of regular contributors who brought to the programme a broad mix of expertise. Among them was Bill Scott, a restaurateur and raconteur who joined me every week to discuss food, drinking and the high-life. But when the mics were off our conversation turned to other matters. Mostly, that meant cars. Fifteen years on, I still count Bill among my closest friends and often call him up to discuss the arrival of a new set of wheels in my life.

There was another contributor who opened my eyes to a whole new set of possibilities. Zog Ziegler, apart from boasting a unique name, fulfilled the role of motoring expert on the programme. He lived far away in Cheltenham, which was near

London as far as I knew then. Every week I would record a chat with Zog down the line from his local radio station in Gloucester. He reviewed cars and discussed motoring-related issues arising in the week. He was exceptionally funny, witty and insightful when it came to pinpointing what it is about a car that makes it useful or hilarious, what it is like to drive, and just what it might mean to own it. This was the first time I had ever encountered a real live motoring journalist and I saw a whole new world open up. Maybe, just maybe, it would be possible for me to do that for a living too.

The idea of driving new cars, formulating opinions on them and then sharing those opinions with an audience struck me as about the most wonderful way possible in which to earn a crust. I live just three or four miles from Zog now and we can still reduce ourselves to tears of laughter or a lather of fury talking about cars. I had watched *Top Gear* every week for as long as I could remember, devoured the weekly and monthly car magazines and stalked the halls at every motor show I could visit. The idea of being involved in the world of motoring as a journalist was like being told as a kid that you could get a job as a jelly-bean taster when you grew up. From the moment I first opened a microphone to talk to Zog, I had a far better idea of what I wanted to do for a living.

Fortunately, the love of cars and bikes that I inherited from my grandfathers didn't extend simply to a passion for posing in them. I'd also inherited a fascination for their innermost workings and a reasonable ability to fettle them when things dropped off or got broken. Which is a good thing to have if you are going to spend your entire life craving cars that are slightly too good for your budget. Every car I bought was a supremely tatty example of its type; it had to be in order for me to afford it. I quickly found that a childhood enjoyment of fiddling with Lego was easily translated into an adult ability to nurse along whatever rusty, broken old nail was the current apple of my car-crazed eye. Sometimes this was just a case of topping up fluids and keeping a set of jump leads handy. Mostly, though, I would find myself attempting to tackle jobs way beyond my wit and tool kit. I wrestled with changing my Mini's engine in a borrowed lock-up using a less sophisticated tool kit than I would expect to be delivered with a flat-pack chest of drawers. I lay in the mud to replace the gearbox under my Cortina-engined kit car through a winter so harsh I would lose all feeling in my back and have to roll on to my knees and crawl inside to get warm. Essentially, my life boiled down to working as a radio reporter and presenter in order to pay for a procession of broken cars which I spent the rest of my time attempting to stick back together so that they could take me to work. That I now own a car capable of reliably travelling tens and even hundreds of miles without incident is still a source of wonder to me.

But there was no more time for ruminating on the past and getting soppy about the cars that had come and gone. Right now I had to walk into a TV studio with all the confidence I could muster to audition for the biggest job opportunity of my life.

I went inside and met the crew who would be filming the audition. I was amazed how many people were involved. When we filmed stuff for Granada Men and Motors there was me and my mate Sid. Suddenly I was in a world of dedicated camera operators, sound technicians, lighting technicians, assistants and assistants to the assistants. I was terrified. And then I was introduced to a man not much taller than me, with a friendly, welcoming face that somehow immediately engenders trust; it turned out to be Andy Wilman. Andy's the man who, along with Jeremy Clarkson, first came up with the idea for a whole new type of car show and persuaded the BBC that it was just what they wanted. I had already spoken to him on the phone when he called to invite me to audition, but this was our first meeting. We had got along instantly on the phone, and our relaxed conversation seemed to continue seamlessly when we met face to face. He took me aside and gave me a pep talk along the lines of 'Try and keep your satellite TV crap out of it, mate. Not too bouncy. This is grown-up TV now, not your Toytown stuff.' The fact that he had given me a few hints about what was wanted filled me with confidence. As far as I was concerned, it meant he was on my side.

It was time to begin. I had been asked to prepare a two-minute piece to present to camera, alone, about a car in the studio. It was a Skoda Superb. I rambled on and wandered around it, pointing out faults and flaws and possible good points, trying to be funny and informative and not to trip over the wires on the floor. The next phase of the audition involved presenting a sequence rather like what is now the news section of *Top Gear*. And for this I would be joined by a legend: Jeremy Clarkson.

To a guy like me, having worked hard to get to the point where he was presenting car programmes on satellite TV, meeting Jeremy was comparable with a rookie racer being invited to drive with Stirling Moss. And I had to meet him for the first time and immediately begin joshing and messing about for the camera. He was turning up for every audition with every candidate so he must have gone through the same process dozens of times. But he couldn't have made it easier or more fun. We argued about cars, discussed favourite motors from our past, took the piss out of motoring stories in the news that week and generally acted up in precisely the way we do on telly now. He laughed at me for being short, I laughed at him for being tall, we both laughed at people who drive electric cars. It was like meeting up with an old mate. We could have conducted the entire conversation sitting on toolboxes with mugs of tea in our hands back at my lock-up. Eventually, though, the audition ended. The next person to be tried out was waiting in the wings, so I had to leave and give him his chance.

Climbing into my car to begin the journey home, I felt no elation at how well it had all seemed to go, but rather a sense of disappointment. I had enjoyed my time with the people in that studio so much that I knew whoever eventually landed the job was going to have a truly fabulous time. Apart from working on what promised to be a brilliant show, they were going to be teamed with a great bunch of people. I just took it for granted that I was never going to be given the role.

I rang Mindy on the way home. She wasn't surprised by my pessimism. She understands me better sometimes than I understand myself.

It was due to my work that Mindy and I first met. After about ten years trying to support myself and my various daft cars and bikes as a freelance radio presenter, I had finally caved in and got a 'proper job' as a PR officer at a corporate headquarters on the outskirts of London. For a brief period I enjoyed earning a reasonable wage. I even enjoyed the commute to work as it covered forty-two miles and I could rely on my brand-new company car to complete it every time without engine fire or oil leaks. In the end, though, the call to return to my chosen career was too strong and I went back into broadcasting. But not before I had found Mindy, who was working in the same office. I took one look at her curves and her long blonde hair combined with an infectious enthusiasm and attitude and ever-present sense of humour and I adored her – and knew that I didn't stand a chance. She has told me since that she took one look at the long-haired, pale-faced, skinny wretch in a cheap suit who turned up one day and decided that I was probably 'interesting'. In fact, we fancied each other from day one.

We took to sneaking off together for fag breaks and spent the time standing about like teenagers at the back of the building while we both tried to think of excuses to spark up another smoke and extend our time together. It was, with hindsight, pretty pathetic; we had both made it fairly obvious that we were interested in meeting outside work, but we lacked the courage to say anything about it.

The breakthrough came when I was given a couple of tickets to a motorsport-related ball. I determined to use them as an excuse to ask Mindy 'out'. Well, I didn't actually do the asking. I recruited the help of the boss's chauffeur, who was duly despatched to tell her that I had a couple of tickets to some party and wondered if she would like to come. It was nothing more than the equivalent of one of those 'my mate really fancies you' conversations from school. It worked though. I picked her up from her flat. She wore a skin-tight, figure-hugging blue dress and I nearly expired with desire when she answered the door. Away from work, our awkwardness disappeared and we spent the evening laughing, talking about music and films and, eventually, snogging like a couple of sixth-formers.

Our follow-up date was spent walking her two beloved dogs.

I remember being amazed that she managed to share a flat the size of a fag packet with a Border collie and a German shepherd, and being touched by the fact that she drove home every lunchtime to walk them rather than leave them alone all day. Our third date was spent at a local horse-riding centre where Mindy displayed the calm accomplishment of a lifelong horse-woman and I bounced around like a monkey riding a piano. For our fourth date, Mindy drove with her dogs out to where I lived on the edge of the Chiltern Hills. We walked over the hills, threw sticks for the dogs, and on the way back we shared a hug. In an instant I fell in love with her. I realised I had met my soulmate and best friend for life.

Mindy's friendship would be sorely tested from the start. She stayed with me when I gave up job security and went back to working in the media, presenting occasional car features on Granada TV's Men and Motors channel. I was once again broke, too broke even to afford a car. Mindy would lend me hers or drop me off at a local garage where I could hire a purple Nissan Micra for a few quid for the day. She helped me with cash and kind words whenever things got tricky and she celebrated with me whenever something came good. We grew closer every year, eventually being blessed with our first daughter, Isabella, and getting married in May 2002.

We had moved to Cheltenham, a beautiful spa town on the edge of the Cotswolds, because Mindy had family in the area and here was a place far enough from London to have its own sense of identity, but not so far as to make travelling to the capital impossible. And now I was heading home with news of yet another audition for yet another job that I wanted more than anything else in the world. I had been told it would be several months before the decision was made, and over that time I became more convinced than ever that I would be getting a call to say thanks but no thanks.

In the event, I was sitting at my desk in the cellar of our house in Cheltenham when the call came. Mindy was down there with me. The phone rang loudly and, for no reason, we were convinced immediately that it was the long-awaited call about the *Top Gear* job. Quite why we should have decided this I have no idea, because the phone rang ten or twenty times a day. But we were right.

Gary Hunter, the executive producer, got straight to the point: 'Hello, Richard. I was wondering – would you like to come and join our team?'

His tone was bright and happy. He was offering me the job I had dreamt of since I was a small child. But what I heard him say was, 'I'm very sorry, but you haven't been lucky this time.' I drew breath, ready to go into my usual speech about being disappointed but hoping that perhaps we might work together one day, and all the other nice stuff you say while your world collapses around you. And then I realised what I had heard. I had got the job. It had dominated our thoughts for the last few months. Now, finally, I had got the call, and the news was unbelievably good.

I put the phone down and looked across at Mindy. 'He said yes. They want me. I got it.'

Mindy was crying. I was shaking.

'Bloody hell. I got it. I actually got it. What do I do now?'

Then I realised that I hadn't managed to ask a single intelligent question about what I would be doing, when I was starting or where I would be based.

'He must think I'm such an idiot. They'll change their minds.'

I called Gary back straight away. Mindy slipped upstairs while I was gabbling on the phone, and after hanging up I wandered off to find her standing in the kitchen. She had fished out a bottle of champagne and was holding it, ready to open.

'Blimey,' I said. 'It's only eleven o'clock. Bit early.'

She looked at me and raised an eyebrow.

'Why not? You're right, let's celebrate.'

We sat in the garden, drank the champagne and talked about what it might mean to us. We had, only a week earlier, agreed the sale of our Cheltenham house and the purchase of a crumbling little place in a remote corner of the Gloucestershire countryside nearby. Would this affect our plans to live in rural splendour with animals around us and space for our daughter – and maybe other children – to grow up? We had no idea yet. There was a lot to unfold with my new job. And most of it really would be brilliant.

Chapter 4

WHAT A JOB!
'I'VE GOT A GREAT IDEA,'
I ANNOUNCED.

No one looked up and I carried on fighting my way through the piles of papers, radio-controlled cars and assorted props that blocked every path through the *Top Gear* office on the fourth floor of the BBC White City building in London. I had burst into the office to find the production team preparing for the ninth series of the show. It was four years since I'd got the call asking me to join *Top Gear* and we had been through a lot together. I hopped up and down like an eager child.

'It's a belter,' I panted. 'Made for the new series. Perfect.'

Andy Wilman looked up from his desk and harrumphed, his normally friendly face creasing into a comically bad-tempered version of itself. He looked like the angry newspaper editor in *Spider Man*. In fact, as *Top Gear*'s editor, he is the man saddled with crafting the mish-mash of daft ideas, dangerous enthusiasms and crazy schemes that float around the *Top Gear* office into a television programme. He is also the man who has to spend a lot of his time keeping BBC executives, the board of complaints, the politically correct lobby, the anti-car lobby and, occasionally, the police at a discreet distance. It was not by accident that his desk was to be found in this cluttered corner. He deliberately sited himself in the midst of the team of researchers, producers, production managers and runners. He had worked his way through the ranks and could do the job of every person in the room if he had to. Which meant there was little they could get away with.

'Listen' – I tried to make it sound commanding but it came out like a plea – 'I just want to go fast. That's it.' I shrugged what I hoped was a dramatic shrug and added in a fake American drawl, 'Jus' real fast.'

I had rehearsed the speech and the sales pitch on the way down the motorway. It had gone better in the car. The show works best when people tip ideas into the mix, so it's not a rare event for someone to stand in front of Andy and try to persuade him that their scheme has the potential to make a great piece of telly. I wasn't nervous about chucking a proposal in, but in this case it was something I really wanted to do and I didn't want the idea to vanish without trace.

'Really, it's that simple,' I ploughed on. 'I don't want to enter a race or do anything complicated. I think we should just do a piece on going faster than we've ever gone before. Straight-line speed, that's the thing. I've driven at two hundred miles an hour in a car and on a bike. What does it feel like to go faster? And I mean a *lot* faster.' I was enjoying the rush as I warmed to my subject. 'Speed can make us feel good. It's a basic caveman desire: to go fast. If you can go really fast then you can catch your dinner and feed your family back in the cave.' I felt I was losing them with the caveman stuff. 'So all we need to do' – trying to make it sound simple now – 'is find something that can go real fast in a straight line. I don't want to set a record. Well, maybe just a record for a car show. We can be the fastest car show on earth. What about that?'

I had caught him. Andy nodded. The team saw the nod and

registered his approval. I knew it would happen. Probably.

In fairness, it wasn't that unusual for one of the team to champion an idea that came in from pretty far outfield. Someone had once suggested that we submerge a car in a tank of water to see how you really escape from a sinking car. That idea got the go-ahead, and sure enough, one cold and damp winter's day, I found myself sitting in an old Vauxhall Carlton suspended from a crane over a special water tank that had been used in several feature films, probably including a James Bond movie or two. We were not making a Bond movie though, we were about to film a demonstration of just how terrifying it is when you find yourself sitting in a car as it sinks and the water laps up and over the windows.

In a typically colourful moment of *Top Gear* genius, just before I climbed into the car the director had shown me a video clip of someone else doing exactly the same thing. Or rather, they had intended doing something similar, but the seasoned stuntman involved had gone into a panic of such intensity that I feared he might die of stress before he got the opportunity to drown. He kicked the windscreen out and escaped to safety through the incoming flood of water.

Snapping back to reality, I tried to remember how to breathe through the diving regulator hidden in the back of the car, gave the thumbs up as cheerily as I could to the stunt crew, and hoped not to be meeting my maker any time soon. It was utterly terrifying. To sit in a car and feel it float, to watch as the water rises up the doors and then the windows until everywhere you turn it's like looking into an aquarium – it's pretty frightening. The water rushed into the car with a threatening roar. It gushed in through the dash, spouting through the air vents. Looking down, it was even more disconcerting to see the water rapidly covering my knees as the car sank.

The light from outside dimmed and turned green as the car sank beneath the surface and the sense of claustrophobia increased as I sat there, knowing that I must wait until the car filled entirely before I opened the doors and scrambled out. The Vauxhall continued to sink, the water now covering the windows completely and rising up the inside to chest height. The central locking clicked over and over as the electrical systems began to short out with the influx of water. I wondered if they would still open when the time came. I rehearsed again the moves needed to spin round and grab the ventilator and air tank hidden in the back. I hoped I wouldn't need them.

As the car filled, the water chased the last air pockets out of remote corners with explosive gurgles and hisses. The whole thing tipped forward as the weight of the engine took the front down first. My chest was soon completely submerged and the water rose up my neck and towards my face. I had rehearsed in my mind the moment when I must sit up straight and push my mouth up to the roof to get a last lungful of air before the car filled with water entirely, but the reality was more frightening than I thought it would be. I was more worried about succumbing to panic and losing control than I was of anything else. If I passed out, if the locks wouldn't open, if the windows caved in under the pressure, we had taken emergency precautions and were ready for that. I had the air tank in the car and a team of emergency divers were on standby and could reach me before I so much as hiccuped or looked uncomfortable. All I had to do was not panic. If I lost it and flailed around like an idiot, it would be harder to rescue me and I would endanger the people around me. I would also look like an utter numpty, and the rest of the team back in the office would never, ever stop taking the piss.

In the event, I kept it together. I sucked in a last breath of air, waited until the car was full and resting on the bottom of the tank, then shoved the door – which opened smoothly – slipped out of the car and bobbed up to the surface like a cork. It was easy. Just don't drive your car into a canal.

The experts told me afterwards that it's all very well waiting until the car hits the bottom, but what if it ends up sitting next to an old fridge and the door won't open? Worse still, another told me that it's not uncommon for police divers to recover a vehicle from a lake and find the door open and the route to safety perfectly clear, but the driver still sitting there, dead, with their seatbelt on, pinning them in place. That's how much of a problem panic can be.

In the four years I had worked on the programme, I had built a reputation for being happy to have a bash at the more risky-seeming stuff. I had absolute faith in the team around me and in their ability to foresee problems. I guess that, really, I was just lucky to be getting paid for exactly the kind of showing off I had been doing all those years ago on my bicycle. So we enjoyed racing a 2CV around Snetterton race track for twenty-four hours, joining the Norwegian Olympic bobsleigh team for a full-speed run down the track in Lillehammer, and running with the bulls in Pamplona.

That came about when I was sent out to record a feature on the new Lamborghini Murcielago roadster in Spain. We decided that the car could provide a massive adrenalin rush and wanted to find something that might give a comparable hit. Running with the bulls was suggested, my hand shot up to volunteer, and the next thing I knew I was standing in a ridiculous pair of white trousers and a red sash in a crammed-full square in Pamplona, waiting for the horns to sound that would indicate that several tons of quite cross bulls had been released on to the streets and it was time to run like hell. In the heavy silence that descended as we waited, nerves frayed and brows sweated. Half the people around me seemed to be over from Ireland in order to fulfil a lifelong ambition. They also seemed still to be drunk from the night before, and the heady scent of strong spirits almost drowned out the deeper smell of sweat.

The streets are cordoned off for the event, with hefty barriers running down each side. I wasn't sure if the fencing was there to keep the bulls out of the watching crowd or us, the runners, in with the bulls. Whatever the original purpose of the barriers, they mean that if you were to change your mind, it would be a bit too late. Much of the route is flanked by buildings as well as barriers, leaving no hope of an escape route.

The adrenalin rush was indeed massive as the klaxon went off and the crowd surged forward. People screamed and just about everyone around me fell over for no discernible reason. The crowd lining the route on the other side of the barriers grew frenetic as the bulls got closer and bore down upon those of us now trapped. The bloke in front of me slipped on the cobblestones and I leapt over his prostrate body. It probably would have been kinder to heft him over my shoulder and carry him to safety, but he was bigger than me and I was in sort of a rush. Another bloke ran towards me, which was strange because it meant he would be running at rather than away from the bulls. Whatever his plan, he interrupted it to grab hold of me by my shirt and throw me into the road. I thought it rather rude at the time, but later, when I watched the event replayed on film, I saw that my back had been inches from the horn tip of one of the bulls. Needless to say, I made it to safety. We spent the rest of the day looning about to see if the Lamborghini could provide a thrill on a par with my bull-running experiences. It didn't.

Someone in the team once suggested we record an item on what happens when a car is struck by lightning. Obviously it would be time-consuming and expensive for me to sit in a car in a field, waiting for lightning to strike. We needed a way to guarantee a strike, and we found it in Germany at a hi-tech research lab where they can generate artificial lightning. Sure enough, I volunteered.

The car sat in a compound surrounded by barbed-wire fences covered in warning signs indicating that trespassers would be fried with millions of volts of electricity before they were prosecuted. The film crew sat around the perimeter wire, the German boffins twirled knobs and inspected dials in the control room, and I sat in the car and wondered what being hit by lightning would feel like. We were about to demonstrate the Faraday cage effect, which dictates that electricity from a lightning strike will travel not straight through the centre of a vehicle – frying everything inside it, including me – but around the metal exterior, making the final leap to the earth from the wheels. The tyres would not be melted, the windscreen would not explode, my hair would not stand on end, and there would be no complicated forms for the director to fill in at the end of the day. It was a scientific fact that this would happen; an absolute. It was as guaranteed as any other scientific law: if I dropped a brick on my head it would hurt; if I placed a ball at the top of a hill it would roll down; if I took water to a hundred degrees it would boil. The lightning would behave in the way predicted because science said so. Nevertheless, sitting in the car as the machines outside hummed and cracked and the boffins read out the millions of volts being prepared especially for me, I felt the familiar grip of nerves. What if the rules of science suddenly changed that day?

Then there was a loud crack, an eerie blue light outside the car, and it was over. Several million volts of Bavaria's best home-made lightning had leapt from the wires overhead, covering the two-metre air gap in a fraction of a second, drawn to the car's metallic body and to the earth waiting below. I said something to camera to the effect of 'If I'm talking to you now without wings and a halo then we have demonstrated that the theory works'. It had, I wasn't dead, so we packed up and went home.

And now I was travelling home once more with news for Mindy of yet another stunt I might be attempting in the name of entertainment. I was pretty sure she would take it well enough. Every one of the stunt-based features I had made had been carefully researched and thoroughly planned, and Mindy knew this. No one in TV takes safety lightly because there is a policy of personal culpability, in principle if not in law. Essentially, if you cock up and someone cops it badly, then as the responsible manager the buck stops with you. You can find yourself in prison if it really is your fault. It's a good system, and it gives reassurance to all of us.

I was, as usual, mobbed by animals and children as soon as I prised open the front door. We had gone ahead and bought our little house in the country when I got the *Top Gear* job and we now shared it with two daughters – Isabella had been joined by her younger sister Willow, now three years old – along with five dogs, three cats, four horses, a small flock of sheep and a handful of chickens. It was a long commute to and from

London, but the reward was a chance to live somewhere we wanted to be. Mindy could not believe that she lived in a place where she could have a horse of her own. Early most mornings, she could be found battling her way up the hills to take food to the sheep, to give the dogs a chance to stretch their legs, or to lead a horse out into the paddock. We indulged our passion for horse-riding, dog-walking and taking the kids out for long rambles in the woods. Mindy had developed a passion for cars almost on a par with mine, and we also rode motorbikes. Mindy passed her bike test in 2005 and I'd surprised her with a Harley of her own on her birthday the following July.

Work made its presence felt, though. There had been times when Mindy found it difficult to watch footage of me doing stunts on *Top Gear*. When we watched the film of the car being dropped into the tank, for instance, I turned to see Mindy sitting with her eyes brimming with tears. She told me that she had been terrified, even though I was sitting there next to her, weeks after the event, and very much not drowned. When the bull-running feature was broadcast she called me a daft sod and warned me about getting myself killed. She was, I think, only half joking.

We spoke briefly that evening about the 'real fast' idea. But it was likely to be a long way off yet and might never become a reality.

Chapter 5

THE JET CAR – JUST ANOTHER DAY AT THE OFFICE

Within twenty-four hours I would be deep in a coma as my damaged brain expanded dangerously within my skull. But right now I was in rural Bedfordshire, crouched in the lee of a Land Rover, picking grass burrs from my dog's coat. It was strangely soothing work, both for the dog and for me, and I let my mind wander back over the day's filming. It had gone well – for a *Top Gear* shoot.

We were working on a sequence in which all three of us decided to try to go green by making our own bio-fuel. To do this, we would need to grow a field full of wheat which could eventually be processed and turned into something that worked very much like diesel. We would start by ploughing, and that meant playing in tractors. James had managed to bury his in a boggy corner of the field; Jeremy had used explosives instead of a plough when he got bored with going slowly; and I had managed to tie my lengthy and very expensive plough in a knot behind my 26-tonne caterpillar-tracked tractor. Earlier in the day I had parked the tractor outside a local newsagent while I nipped inside to buy a proper ploughman's lunch for the team. It was a very, very big tractor, and when I dashed out of the shop with a carrier bag full of cheese and pickled onions, I discovered that my enormous machine had blocked the only street of the village. A man driving a bus was swearing under his breath, a lady in a BMW was swearing out loud, and every curtain at every window in the street was twitching as the residents watched a red-faced man off the telly trundle off down the narrow street, just missing the cars parked on either side.

Top Gear Dog – or TG as she is known – had enjoyed her day hugely. We had wheeled her out for duty as a sheepdog, to clear the sheep from the field before our ploughing attempts could begin. We were hoping she wouldn't be much good and it would provide a moment of light relief for the viewer before we got stuck in to the main business of the day. She didn't disappoint; she was spectacularly bad at being a sheepdog. Half of the problem stemmed from the fact that with her pale woolly coat she looks rather like a sheep anyway so our targets felt perfectly at home in her company. Instead of fleeing from her in terror into the neighbouring field like we wanted them to, they were happy to nod at her in a friendly way before getting back to chewing the grass. We ran, slipped and fell over in the mud and were laughed at for a good half-hour or so before a proper shepherd arrived with his two Border collies.

When Jeremy's explosives were due to be detonated, I took TG off to a safe distance and sat with her, ready to offer comfort and calming words when the moment came. They went off with seven or eight dull thuds that you felt through the ground as much as heard. Every crow for about a thousand miles around lifted off from its branch and a shower of dirt and small stones rained down. TG looked at me, put her head down on her paws and went back to sleep. She's not easily flustered.

She was due to come with me to York after we finished

filming; I'd thought it might add a rather jolly pilot-style flavour to the whole thing, having the dog standing on the airfield while I drove the jet car. We had rung ahead and the people at the hotel were happy to let her kip in my room, even though they didn't usually allow dogs. So when we finished filming the final sequence of the day I went over to collect TG. I knew something was wrong as soon as I saw her. Clearly, she had spent the afternoon tearing up and down the fringes of the fields, where her long woolly coat had picked up several million spiky grass burrs. These had so embedded themselves in her fur that they were causing her some discomfort as she wriggled around and tried to remove them. I picked as many from her as I could, but it was hopeless. I rang Mindy and we agreed that there was only one alternative. A member of the production team would drive her back home, where an expert would make sure all the burrs were removed. She wasn't going to be coming to York and she would miss the jet car. And I would miss her. A photograph of me sitting on the ground with her and picking those grass burrs from her coat would feature in several newspapers over the next few weeks.

The various crews were packing up their kit and readying themselves to head off to different locations for film shoots the next day. When we are getting ready for a new series, everyone works hard to get as many of the films made as possible before we all get tied up with recording the studio element of the programme. Camera operators and sound recordists might be filming Jeremy hurtling around the test track in a Lamborghini one day, a race between one of us in an off-roader and a guy on a mountain bike down a muddy hill the next day, and all three of us sinking in a lake while trying to make cars amphibious the next. It keeps them on their toes. James and Jeremy were heading off to their shoots, and we all knew that we would talk on our phones the following day to moan about how the weather was ruining our filming or to boast about how brilliantly it was going.

Jeremy asked me what I was going to do. I told him it was the jet-propelled car thing up at Elvington.

'Oh, you're actually driving it then?'

'Yes.'

'Goodbye,' he said as he extended his hand with an air of absolute finality, as one might to a man walking to the gallows. It was a pretty standard joke, the sort of thing we all do among ourselves on a daily basis. He was making out that I was sure to be 'killed to death' in a horrible crash.

'Yeah, whatever. It'll be fine.'

I phoned home and spoke to Mindy. She had picked up Izzy from school and Willow from nursery and we spoke about their day. Izzy was breathless and excited as always, telling me about her swimming lesson, the fabulous lunch that she had eaten seconds of, and how many times she had run round the field afterwards. When I spoke to Willow, she giggled, shouted at her big sister for pushing her, and said goodbye almost as soon as she had said hello. I felt a pang as I pictured them in the kitchen, helping Mindy tidy away the tea plates before a last-minute play and then bedtime. Sometimes, missing them becomes a real physical sensation in my chest that takes my breath away. On *Top Gear* shoots when we are all away from home, there comes a period at about seven in the evening when Jeremy, Andy Wilman, me and any other members of the crew with young families can be found on our own with a mobile phone glued to our ear wishing our kids goodnight. No matter how much fun we have when we are away working, there are moments when we all regret not being at home to tuck our kids in and give them a goodnight kiss. Of course, we would never normally share this feeling back at the shoot or in the hotel bar. But we all know it goes on.

It was at least three hours to the hotel in York. Because of my job, I drive a lot of different cars in order to be able to write a script before filming them for *Top Gear* or review them for my column in the *Mirror*. On this occasion I had borrowed a Honda S2000 two-seater roadster. I was glad of the distraction of a test car to drive and spent much of the journey planning what I would write when I got back after the following day's filming.

It was a long way, but the weather was kind, the roads weren't too badly clogged with evening traffic, and I had the radio for company. Settling into the driver's seat, I turned my thoughts to the jet car I would be driving the following day. We had done a lot of research on it and had prepared a great script for the shoot. It wasn't about the absolute speed so much as the sensation of driving a jet-powered car with 10,000 bhp. I tried to imagine unleashing the power of eleven Formula One cars in one huge hit of adrenalin-bursting speed and couldn't get anywhere near. I concentrated on the road ahead, illuminated by my headlights. I watched the trees and lamp-posts whizzing by on either side and tried to multiply that speed by a factor of three or four. I just couldn't imagine it. This would be a whole new experience and would, I suspected, forever change my idea of what it meant to go fast.

Over the past few weeks we had talked a lot about how to make the best of this opportunity to drive a pretty special machine. We had all agreed that it would be best not to get too caught up on the numbers. This was going to be a film about how it felt rather than just about how fast it could go. As someone who has driven just about every performance car and supercar on the market, competed in a few races and hurtled up runways in some special kit before, but never had a taste of jet power, it would be an interesting experiment. If I spent too much time staring at the speedo and trying to squeeze an extra couple of miles an hour out of the car before I ran out of runway to drive on, there was a real danger that I might get something wrong, and that could be disastrous. Anyway, driving a car with that kind of power, we knew it would be going plenty fast enough for our purposes. The best way, we decided, was for there to be no speedo in the car and for no one on the day to tell me how fast I had gone. We would know the figures from the on-board telemetry system, which would record the speed of the car, the acceleration, the g-forces and every single input I made into the controls as I drove. But that information would be referred to in the studio, after I had driven the car and put it safely away again. I would be taught how to drive it by the man who had built it and drove it regularly at drag strips and events all over the country and beyond. I would progress slowly, increasing the power and, of course, the speed as the day progressed and at a pace that both the owner and I were happy with.

A mate of mine, Colin Goodwin, a motoring journalist, had already driven the exact same car. Colin's down-to-earth explanation had been very useful in researching for the piece we were filming and, of course, in satisfying my curiosity about what lay ahead of me. It was, he had told me, mind blowing. He had hit over 270 mph and never again looked at speed in quite the same way. He assured me that the machine was actually simple enough to operate and reckoned I was in for a pretty fantastic time and would love my day in a jet car. A technical expert had been despatched from the BBC to give the car a thorough check and to make sure everything was in order. It was. The car looked great and I was looking forward to driving it.

By seven o'clock I was rolling into York and getting horribly lost in the maze of one-way systems. I lived and worked in York for two or three years but can no more navigate my way around it today than I could find my way across Tokyo without a map. I eventually found my way to the hotel. The next day's film crew had arrived and were settled in to the bar for a last pint before bed. The team who had brought the car were also present. Colin Fallows, the guy who had built it, was in a corner and I sat next to him, eager to learn more about what was to come the following day.

I enjoyed our chat. As a technical man and a keen driver, Colin was someone I was bound to get on with. He had served extensively in the RAF and worked with jet engines for decades, and was a fund of stories, anecdotes and technical insights on the subject of jets, planes and, of course, jet-propelled dragsters. I was surprised and charmed by his quiet manner. I had expected some gung-ho type full of bravado but found that Colin displayed the opposite traits. We quickly settled in to a friendly conversation about how he had built the car and why. I looked at him, a small, slightly portly chap who looked more like a bank manager or quantity surveyor than a man who habitually took the helm of a dragster that propelled him to speeds in excess of 300 mph. It goes to show that you really never can tell about people until you talk to them.

I slipped away to bed early. In my room, I found that a tartan dog bed and metal food bowl had been laid out ready for TG, who by now would be back with Mindy rather than lurking by my side. It made me sad to see this reminder that my dog couldn't be with me. I rang Mindy. TG was fine and was booked in to visit the groomer tomorrow morning. The children were sleeping soundly and soon she would be too. We wished each other goodnight. The following day was shaping up to be an exciting one and I was looking forward to it. Very soon, the jet-car drive would be behind me and I would be setting off home again. But first, sleep.

Chapter 6

20 SEPTEMBER 2006

I fished an arm under the bed and stretched my fingers out, feeling for my quarry. The car keys could have dropped off the bedside table in the night and somehow rolled under the bed. But I couldn't find them. I had got to the room door, my bags hanging from my shoulder and my coat over my arm, ready to go, before I realised something was missing. And now time was pressing. I had already decided to forgo the hotel breakfast; I knew that I could breakfast later on at the airfield while the crew rigged their kit and we made ready for the first shots of the day. All I had to do was find the flaming keys before dashing down to the garage.

I stamped over to the door and bent to pick up my canvas shoulder bag. I knew it was the action of an obsessive and nervous bloke, but I figured it was worth checking it just once more in case the keys lurked within the bag and had been missed on my first sweep of the pockets. Sure enough, I found them in the front pocket. I felt that surge of relief at finding something you had thought lost, closely followed by another surge, this time of anger at myself for being such a disorganised clot. Grabbing my bags, I hefted the door open and ran.

It was not an easy feat of navigation, but somehow our tiny

convoy made it to Elvington. A base had been set up at one end of the main runway and our collection of cars and crew vans were gathered on a concrete apron. Surrounding the airfield, I saw stretches of dark green coniferous forest in the distance. The land was flat and broad and a light wind blew across it under a pale blue sky. I made my way towards the small crowd assembled round some sort of catering van. I recognised Scott, the director, and said good morning.

'Seen the car yet?' he asked.

'Nope. Can't wait. Where's Colin?'

'Getting it ready. They'll bring it over in a sec.'

I ordered a cup of tea and a bacon sarnie. We've adopted a sort of military approach to eating on these shoot days: if you see food, eat it, because you might not get a chance later.

With a cup of hot tea in my hand, I sought out Scott again and we got our heads together for a brief planning session. There was much to do, but for once we had to do it at the natural pace at which events unfolded. We couldn't force anything. I had to be introduced to the car, and taught how to drive it. This would take as long as it took. We had a few bits to film where I would talk to camera about the car and how it was made, but we decided to do that at the end of the day. We only had the runway until 5.30 p.m., after which time noise restrictions would end our chances of driving the car. By saving some of the links until after we had done all the driving stuff, we could make the best use of the day.

I grabbed another cup of tea and sat in the Honda, reading through the script. There's only so much you can write before you make a feature like this one, but we could structure it pretty rigidly and knew the main points. The only bits to be sketched in on the day would be my responses to driving the car. We wanted to record how it felt, what went through my mind, and how it related to driving the other fast cars I have driven.

I rang Andy Wilman back in London. We stay in constant touch when we're out filming, and it's useful to speak with someone away from the scene of the actual shooting, who can retain a sense of perspective. Andy reiterated the importance of not getting caught up in talking about specific speeds. We agreed that this was all about the sensation of driving the thing. I told him that I would call him back as soon as I had completed my first drive.

Before I even got to sit in the Vampire, let alone interfere with the controls, Colin was going to take it for a shakedown blast up the runway. This was, I suspected, the only way that Colin's mind could be put at rest that everything was working OK. It was the sort of hands-on approach you would expect from him. The car appeared, being towed up to our end of the runway, and I got my first look at it. I was surprised by how long it was. It was more like the top-fuel dragsters I had loved when I was a kid. I would rummage about in my huge tub of Lego to build drag racers that looked exactly like the Vampire, with its long, skinny body, big chunky rear wheels and skinny little front ones. But my models had never had the strange cylindrical metallic addition that lay immediately behind the driver's head. This was the jet engine, the heart of the machine and the very reason for its existence.

Colin was in the driver's seat and he steered the thing into position on the start line. We had gathered a couple of hundred metres away, along the edge of our concrete apron. Colin's technical assistant hopped out and busied himself making adjustments and checks that I didn't understand but guessed were important. Our whole team watched in silence. These technical checks went on for just long enough for my mind to begin running over what lay ahead of me that day. This was a new world to me, with engines that worked differently from the ones I knew and understood.

Eventually, I picked out the unmistakable whine of a jet engine starting up. The whine built to a shriek and the support guy got out of the way. We waited, our own tension growing with the noise from the engine. Hot air shimmered dizzyingly around the back of the car where the massive engine's thrust poured out into the crisp autumn morning. Then, with no warning, the car leapt forward. There was a burst of flame from the engine's outlet at the back and a roar as the noise hit us. Colin was using the afterburners, so this would be a full-power run – I knew that much from our conversation the previous evening. I tried to imagine what it must feel like, being hit in the back by a 10,000 horsepower engine and shooting up to 300 mph in the time it takes a fast road car to hit sixty. Watching from the sidelines, the car's acceleration seemed endless. It gained speed with a relentless effortlessness that suggested it might keep getting faster and faster until it just disappeared. And then, only a few seconds after it set off, we could see in the distance the parachute mushrooming behind the car and then the noise from the engine dwindled and vanished. Silence descended on us as the parachute collapsed to the ground behind the now stationary car half a kilometre or so down the runway. This was showing off on a grand scale, and I understood precisely why people do it. But I felt a twinge of nerves in the pit of my stomach. That had looked like a very great deal of power being unleashed to catapult a very small car up a very short runway.

It took half an hour for the car to be made safe and towed

back up to the launch point. While Colin and his team did technical stuff, we loitered by the burger van. The guys were asking how it felt, knowing that I was going to be driving the same car. I told them I was nervous, but pretty sure we could manage it. I've spent too much of my life standing around waiting to do things that have made me nervous to be caught out by nerves now. It's best to be aware of the nerves, to feel them but not to let them take over and affect you. The nerves help by sending adrenalin flooding around your body, making you sharper and your responses faster; but if you let them take over your mind then you can lose focus. And there was something strangely comforting about feeling nervous that day. Because it was a familiar sensation it gave me a sense of consistency, taking me back to my first radio show or my first daft stunts on bicycles. I put the nerves to one side and ordered another cuppa.

Soon enough, the car was ready. Colin and I walked towards it together, leaving the crew behind. We would film a TV version of our briefing later on, but this was the real thing and best done without having TV cameras stuck in our faces. Colin began to fill me in on what the car could do and how it went about doing it. We laughed and joked as he explained that the engine was mounted in such a way that the thrust it provided also pressed it down on to the tarmac. This was achieved by having the jet point up a couple of degrees at the back, so it shoved the car very slightly downwards as well as forwards. This put my mind at rest a little about the dangers of the engine suddenly trying to revert to its former life of sending an aeroplane hurtling around the skies. Then Colin indicated that it was time for me to climb in.

The narrow aperture into the cockpit meant I had to slide

myself in carefully, ducking my head beneath the protective bars of the rollover structure. I settled into the hard seat and felt the dense, wide webbing of the harness behind my back. I tugged the straps so that they fell in front of me, draping across my shoulders and chest. When I did this for real, the harness would be tightly fastened down to keep me firmly in place if anything went wrong.

Colin talked me through the controls. There were surprisingly few. Essentially, the car consists of an engine, a parachute and the seat. Because the engine does not transmit the power to the road, there are no complicated systems for sending the power through the wheels. It just revs up and sends the thrust out of the hole at the back. Because it's bolted to the engine, the car is thrown forward with it. So there is a control for turning the engine up to the required level in much the same way that you set the volume on a radio. The metal dial, about the size of the base of a teacup, sat on the right-hand side of the rudimentary dashboard. Just below the engine control was a large metal lever, hinged beneath the dash. Colin explained that this cut the engine and deployed the parachute simultaneously. This, then, was my main braking system. Once under way in earnest, the brakes on the wheels would be useless against the huge thrust from the engine and I would rely on the 'chute to bring everything to a halt. In the centre of the metal dash panel was the steering wheel. This was of the 'butterfly' type, made up of two small handles, each like the end of a garden spade, connected in the centre at a metal boss about four inches across. I immediately liked it for its dramatic shape, tiny proportions and businesslike finish. This was not a wheel you'd find fitted to anything ordinary. I rested my hands on the two handles, feeling the cool bare metal.

Through this wheel would be transmitted the results of all the power unleashed by the massive engine just a couple of feet behind my head.

I looked around the cramped cockpit. These were all the controls I had to operate, then. There was no clutch pedal because there was no clutch. There was no accelerator because I dialled the power in before I set off and then left the dial alone. My right foot rested next to the footbrake, which was used only to hold the car stationary as the engine got up to speed. My left foot would rest on a dead man's pedal, which cut the engine the moment my foot released it. This was a device that would come into action only in an emergency.

It was not the interior I'd imagined. I had envisaged rows of toggle switches controlling any number of intricate functions. I had seen myself confidently flicking switches to operate complex systems to meet the Vampire's insatiable appetite for fuel and air. I expected to see every surface sprouting more switches, the gaps between them filled by gauges and dials. But what I found was a collection of controls as simple as the ones on the plastic dashboard I had stuck to the back of my dad's driving seat as a kid. There are more systems to monitor on a family hatchback. I was slightly disappointed but also reassured that if this was all I had to concentrate on, there would be little to distract me from the business of steering and stopping at the right point.

I stared down the runway stretching off to the tree-lined horizon. I imagined how it might feel. When Colin gave the signal, I would take my foot off the brake and feel the car surge forward with unimaginable force. Would it be smooth and steady, or would my head be jostled around, making it hard to see ahead? Would the g-force snap my head back? Would I have to do much steering through the tiny, weird-shaped wheel to keep it going straight ahead? I asked Colin how I used the afterburner. He told me that we would not get round to using that until later, but when I did it was just a case of thumbing the innocuous metal switch on top of the left-hand grip on the steering wheel. When I hit the switch, a flame would be sent shooting down the centre of the engine behind me, igniting the unburned fuel in the engine and turning it into something like a cross between a standard jet engine and a rocket. The power would instantly be doubled.

'Do I hit the button as I take my foot off the brake, or do I set off and then hit it?'

'You take your foot off the brake and then hit the button.'

'What if my foot is still on the brake?' I didn't want to get it wrong.

'Makes no difference. When you hit that button, you are going that way.' Colin pointed up the runway.

'Right.' I felt like a ten-year-old.

Before I did my first run, we would record a couple of bits of telly about the car and what I was there to do that day. It would be no good speculating on camera about how it might feel to drive the Vampire if I was dripping with sweat from having already done it. I would get changed into my driving kit, knock off a couple of pieces to camera, and then get on with the serious business of the day – the driving.

Another member of the *Top Gear* production team, Grant Wardrop, had joined us for the day. It was unusual for him to get out of the office but he had been heavily involved in setting this one up and it was useful for him to be with us on the ground. He passed me one bag stuffed with a set of racing overalls, boots and gloves, and another containing a crash helmet. I protested that I had brought my own helmet with me, but he insisted that I use the one provided. He had realised early on that this was a pretty unique drive and had personally researched the best crash helmet for the job. And now he insisted that I wore it.

There was nowhere to get changed. I asked the paramedic guys if I could borrow their ambulance and turn it into a dressing room. They agreed that I could, as long as I didn't fill it full of flowers and blue M&Ms. I laid the silver-coloured racing suit out on the trolley bed and inspected the kit more closely. The suit was made of thick fire-retardant material and the label told me that it was four layers dense. I pulled it on over a T-shirt and underpants and knew instantly that I looked ridiculous. The boots only made it worse. They were a bit too clean and well presented to be the boots of a jet-car veteran. They were more pixie than pole position. At the bottom of the bag I found the neck brace, a circle of padding that sits immediately below the opening of the helmet and limits how much your head can move in a crash. I put it on and doubted that the big blue circle just below my chin had improved an already shaky image.

The helmet, though, was a beauty. It was a plain white Arai, built specifically for car racing, and there was an air of quality to it. I've ridden motorcycles for twenty-odd years so a new crash helmet holds a particular appeal. I grabbed it by the chin-guard and hopped out of the ambulance's back doors. Predictably, the crew laughed when I came into view. I looked like an extra from an early episode of *Doctor Who*, with my spangly silver race suit, blue neck brace and racing bootees. I adopted a Superman flying pose and, declaring myself to be the Silver Flash, asked if someone could sort me a cuppa before

I set off to save a dog that was trapped down a well, and put out a forest fire.

The car was waiting for me on the start line and it was time to get to work. The crew were despatched to their pre-appointed vantage points around the runway and busied themselves getting cameras and sound-recording equipment ready. There were cameras on board the car too, tiny digital ones mounted so that they could look back at my face and forward along the length of the car.

As far as I was concerned, though, this part of the day was not about the filming. My role now was not TV presenter but jet-car driver. I replayed Colin's patient and thorough explanation of what I must do and put one hand on the side of the car, ready to climb in. Colin was there to remind me of the routine. I climbed over the side of the car. Colin glanced in, looked around to check that everything was OK, and stepped back to allow his technician to fasten the harnesses. They were pulled tight; so tight that I could barely breathe. These guys were not taking any chances. And then Colin leaned in again and began fastening straps that connected my upper arms to the harness.

'What are they for?' I asked.

'If you have a crash, they stop your arms from flailing around.'

I looked to the side at the massive roll bars and winced as I imagined trapping an arm between one of them and the ground.

Colin asked me to run through the controls with him again. This time, though, it was no dry run. When I asked for air and power, the engine would be started for real and I would be at the controls of a running jet engine for the first time in my life. Making a conscious effort to breathe steadily, I went through the motions one last time. I made no wisecracks now, there was no larking about; there was simply an atmosphere of calm and seriousness as we got ready. With Colin happy, we were ready to do it for real.

I called for air and power. Colin flicked the switches. Immediately behind my head, an engine capable of delivering enough power to shove a jet fighter around the skies woke up and began to turn. Despite knowing exactly what was going on, how the engine worked and what would happen next, I felt a surge of excitement mixed with fear as my mind was invaded by the very close presence of a jet engine. The sound rose to the shriek familiar to us all from airports across the world. But on this occasion I wasn't settling into a seat and fastening my belt, there were no other passengers around me, and there was no one else to control the massive engine that was now increasing in volume. As the noise rose to a howl, Colin gave the thumbs up and looked at me. I signalled that all was well and he walked backwards to the starting position, just ahead and to my right.

My foot was holding the car in place, and I could feel it straining against the brake. The car, which until now had been tended and ministered to like a delicate patient, had been transformed into a wild creature, held back just by my right foot. Colin signalled that I should go. This was it. I lifted my foot away from the brake.

The acceleration was massive. I had expected a mind-warping blur of speed as I exploded away from the line, but this was different, a firm and insistent shove that I had no choice but to go along with. The speed increased. Fast. Within 13.7 seconds of taking my foot off the brake, I had passed 205 mph. But there was no way of knowing that inside the cockpit. And even if there had been a speedo fitted, I would have hesitated to lower my eyes and glance at it. There was a lot to do. I was making constant corrections, struggling to keep the car heading straight ahead. Because of the camber of the airfield and the crosswind, I had been told to apply a constant thirty degrees of steering input in order to keep the car going straight. I had not anticipated how much this was needed. Perhaps because of the enormity of the engine, the power and the noise going on at the back of the car, I had not really thought about how busy it might get at the front. Far from being the brave but pointless passenger I had thought I would be, I found that the driver in this instance was a very, very busy individual.

I tried to keep my eyes focused on the track ahead. Very soon I would pass the traffic cones that signalled the point at which I must shut down the engine and deploy the parachute to stop. It was hard to see. The runway surface communicated every bump and ripple through the wheel. The car itself shifted and vibrated. The noise now was all-pervading. My senses were swamped by a constant scream as the engine hurtled me towards the horizon.

As we charged forward, my crash helmet was buffeted by a wind of unimaginable force. It bounced my head around, adding to the disorientation. For a brief second I wondered what would happen if I missed the cones. To make matters worse, my visor was steaming up. Perhaps my neck brace was acting as a seal around the bottom of the helmet, stopping the exhaled air from escaping. Perhaps I was breathing too much, with the exertion of steering, and the excitement. I tried to control my chest, pacing my breaths, feeling my throat shiver and contract as I tried to breathe out slowly and calmly. The visor misted more. I couldn't lift a hand from the wheel to fiddle for the latch and open it. And even if I could, I didn't fancy a face full of wind at whatever speed I was now travelling. And then, through the misted visor, I saw the cones just ahead. It was time.

As the runway hurtled past at God knows what speed, I moved my hand away from the wheel and found the lever to the right. I pulled it and the jet engine changed from a shrieking monster to a calmer, more docile beast as its furious howls relaxed into a lengthy sigh. I wondered if the parachute had worked. And then I was shoved forward in my seat and I knew that the huge silk canopy had fired out of its tube at the back of the car and now grabbed at the air moving by at 206 mph.

The tug from the parachute was astonishing. At full acceleration, a car like this might manage to shove the driver into the seat with 1.8 g. That's 1.8 times the force of gravity, compared to the 0.5 g a road-going sports car might manage. Under braking, though, the huge parachute canopy can arrest the car so that the driver is thrown forward with 3.5 g compared to the most a normal car driver is ever likely to feel under braking of 1 g. It took my breath away as I strained forward against the tight harnesses. But it felt good. It was the finale, the last act in a drama lasting just seconds but taking in forces so incredible they seemed to belong to another world.

In 9.3 seconds, the car slowed to a more pedestrian 60 mph. I steered to the left and headed to the point where I knew the crew would be expecting me to stop. We had planned for the end of this first run. Having filmed the car as it hurtled up the runway, they would dash over to a pre-arranged spot where it would come to rest and I would deliver a few words about how it had felt. I didn't bother planning what I would say. This was one occasion when it is best to just open your mouth to allow whatever is in your mind to flood out. The results may not be considered and eloquent, but they will be heart-felt and honest. And as a viewer, that gives you something more special and more personal than the most polished and considered speech. It's when TV really can take you somewhere.

The film crew dashed towards me, with the director, Scott, at the head of the group. As soon as the camera looked settled, I started talking. I blurted out words, trying to convey the exhilaration, the excitement; trying to communicate how it had felt to be totally at the whim of something so incredibly powerful for a few brief seconds. My mate Colin Goodwin had told me how his drive in the same car had been a life-changing experience. I knew now what he meant by that. It was only one o'clock. I wanted to go faster, I wanted more speed. I knew that I would get it before the day was out.

It had been an overwhelming experience that turned out to be every bit as adrenalin-charged as I'd expected. But it was an experience that was due to be repeated several times that day – I was scheduled to make a further five or six runs – and there was much work to be done. I clambered out of the car and spent a moment or two with Colin Fallows. He had driven this car thousands of times and I looked into his eyes to try to catch a glint of recognition that we two had now shared an experience and visited a place not visited by many.

Over yet another cup of tea, I cornered Pat, the producer, and told him about the problems with the visor. We rang the production team and set them looking for a local shop where we could buy one of a number of products that spray on to the inside of helmet visors and stop them from steaming up. Within minutes, the researchers back at the office had found such a place and an on-site researcher was standing by to make the dash. But I knew of a simpler solution. Smearing a tiny spot of washing-up liquid on to the surface of the visor has exactly the same effect. It's an old biker's trick, and it works. While it might be cooler somehow to despatch a researcher who would return with a glitzy pot of spray-on demister, it was quicker to pop over to the control tower and ask to borrow a bottle of Fairy.

I had recently taken up smoking again after several years of abstinence. It had happened on another *Top Gear* shoot when we had been chased across Alabama by angry rednecks after we painted slightly rude slogans down the sides of our cars. They pursued us in pick-ups with shotguns. We fled across two states, only stopping when we reached the safety of our motel. I ended that day by sparking up my first cigarette in three years, and right now seemed like a good moment to indulge too. I slipped quietly into the peace and solitude of the waiting Honda press car, sparked up a smoke and sat back. I felt good. I had known all along that driving the jet car would be fine, that I would be nervous but then elated and in control. And that was exactly how it had turned out. With the first run out of the way, the rest would be more enjoyable.

There was much still to do. We had to film pieces to camera with me explaining how the car worked, and we had to film more shots of the car in action. More to the point, I still had to progress to using the afterburner and do a full-bore run with all 10,000 bhp unleashed behind me. This would happen only when, and if, Colin judged I was ready. I was pretty sure that he would give me the go-ahead and I was looking forward to the experience. Driving the same car but with twice the power would be a huge buzz. I reminded myself that the run I had completed had only been the first step on a big ladder.

I rang home to speak to Mindy. I knew she was worried and

tried my best to reassure her that it was no big deal and everything was under control. I then phoned Andy Wilman to let him know that the first run had gone well and I had not flashed past the waiting cameras as a flaming fireball. We joked and messed about, but I could tell that he was genuinely relieved that we had everything under control.

The walkie-talkie in the Honda yelped into life. I was wanted – duty called. I hauled myself out of the car and strode across the airfield; a man in his thirties, living the dream he'd had since childhood. I was walking confidently towards a jet-propelled car which I would be driving in front of not only an assembled TV crew but, thanks to the efforts of that crew, hundreds of millions of TV viewers the world over. It doesn't do to get too self-congratulatory in life – pride comes before a fall and all that – but as I walked across the smooth tarmac and slipped the neck brace on to the shoulders of my silver racing suit, the ten-year-old boy still living inside me was giggling with excitement and bursting with pride.

After a pep talk with Colin, I made my second run. I thrilled to the sensation of the power and the speed, and hopped about in front of a TV camera afterwards, trying to convey a sense of what I was experiencing. And then I did it again. By now it was well past midday and the crew had been working hard all morning. We had filmed the beginning of the piece and several runs in the car. The next thing was for me to try a run with the afterburner lit. But first, lunch, which on the TV shoots I find myself on is likely to consist of whatever we can grab from a petrol station and force into our faces between takes. It was a delight to us all to find that the same van that had fuelled us with bacon sarnies that morning had now turned itself to knocking out burgers at a rate that even a hungry TV crew could not outstrip. It was genuinely heart-warming to see the guys getting to feast on real food for once. It was even more heart-warming to get to the front of the queue and put in my order for a burger with cheese, onions and anything else the lady behind the counter could fry.

'We'll get soft if we get treated like this too often,' I muttered to no one in particular through a mouthful of burger bun.

I rang Andy again, and told him that I would be trying the afterburner next. He reminded me that I had to go at my own pace. I reassured him that I would only do what I felt was safe to do.

Back in the jet car, I studied the switch that operated the afterburner. It was a tiny metal thing, exactly the sort of hardware knick-knack that would lie at the back of a kitchen drawer for years before being slung out with the expired ball-points and plug adaptors that accumulate in odd corners. It was a frankly rather cheap means of initiating a procedure that would unleash quantities of power that for millennia were seen as the preserve of the gods.

Colin described the process. A flame would shoot down the centre of the engine and ignite unburned fuel. The power output of the mighty jet engine would, effectively, be instant-aneously doubled. I rehearsed the moment many times: start the engine, look straight ahead, hit the button as my foot came off the brake and then, seconds later, pull the 'chute and celebrate being alive.

The jet engine whined into life and built in a screaming crescendo. I looked across at Colin, who gave me a confident smile. I took a deep breath, stared straight ahead and flicked the button as I lifted the brake pedal. I sensed, rather than heard, the roar. Something more than the engine kicked me in the back. The car jolted forward, but then it settled into something more familiar. I knew immediately that something had gone wrong with the afterburner. Perhaps it had gone out like a pilot light on a central-heating boiler? At the end point, Colin was ready to answer my questions. The afterburner had lit, briefly, but had failed to catch and deliver the proper effect. So it was back to the start line and a second chance to do it properly.

The same procedure, the same intense noise building behind me. Colin stepped back into position and gave me the thumbs up. I knew enough now to realise that this would be a very different experience from the runs I had completed so far. I took in a deep breath, hit the button to fire the afterburner and lifted my right foot to release the brake.

I was suddenly in a different car. I heard the roar and felt acceleration like I had never felt before. This time, the car exploded into action. This was like pulling up a chair at the very front of an explosion and then riding it towards the horizon. I realised now that the jet engine without the afterburner was a friendly, amiable beast that put a hand at my back and pushed me gently up the runway as an adult might push along a child's toy car. This, though, was a manic, violent thing. I can't say that it really felt any different from a fast drive in a supercar, but I was aware at the same time that it was different. I could sense that my mind and my senses were operating at optimum speed to act fast enough to cope with and stay alert to what was happening.

In just 17.2 seconds I drew level with the cones that signalled the end of the run. I pulled the lever to cut the engine and deploy the 'chute. Just twenty-three seconds after hitting that innocuous little button on top of the steering wheel, the run was finished. I had ridden a wave of power that ten Formula One cars together would struggle to achieve. I felt more alive, more vital than I could remember feeling in a very long time. Colin was happy, the crew were happy, the director was happy, and I was ecstatic. On that run I had hit 314.4 mph – faster than the official British Land Speed Record, though it would never be recognised as an official record because we had no official referees or monitors present from the record books. And anyway, no one was going to tell me how fast I had gone just in case I suddenly decided to try to go a little faster.

Back at the tea van there was lots of excited chatter. Things were looking good: we had plenty of footage of Colin showing me around the car, plenty of shots of my first attempts without the afterburner, and now, shots of my full-bore afterburner run too. I rang Andy and we agreed that this was going to be a good old-fashioned piece of family telly where a guy learns how to do something scary and we all get to watch as he does it.

It was now fast approaching five p.m. We only had permission to use the runway until 5.30, when local agreements meant the noise had to be cut. We talked it over. The car was running well, I was on top of controlling it, the weather was perfect. There was, we reckoned, just time for one more run.

While the guys prepped the car and the crew got into position, I chatted with the man in charge of the runway. The sun drifted towards the horizon enough to turn the light a gentle red, and a soft peace fell over the pastoral scene. We agreed that the weather had been great all day and that the car was an amazing thing. He already knew that we wanted to do just one more run, but I wanted to make sure he was happy and assured him that we would get it over with and then cut the noise for the day. Back with the director, we reminded ourselves that we also had one more lengthy piece to camera to record, in which I had to walk around the car, describing how it worked. But that, we decided, could be done after the 5.30 p.m. noise curfew. Best use the noise-making time we had left to make noise.

Time: 17.25

After the crash, some doctors felt that the degree of recollection I had of events running up to it were unrealistically clear. Perhaps, they reckoned, these memories were the product of an active imagination that had cobbled them together as I lay in a coma. But I remain convinced that they are real. They certainly tally perfectly with the records of the on-board telemetry system that can account for every millisecond and millimetre of the crash as it happened.

Walking towards the car for what I knew would be the final time, my mind wandered briefly back to a conversation with a race technician just a few weeks earlier. He had warned me never to race with a full bladder. 'You race when you need a piss and there's a chance that, if you crash, your bladder could burst. And then you'll be dead before the medics get to you. Why do you think F1 drivers pee in their race suits if they need to go?' Suddenly, just a few feet from the Vampire, I turned round and hiked back to the blue plastic Portaloo a hundred metres away. I do not believe that this was any sort of premonition or vision of what was about to unfold. I just needed a piss so I took one before I did something that would, I knew, demand a clear head and full concentration.

I looked at the car as I slotted my neck brace round my neck. The brakes had originally come from a Transit van. The fuel pump came from a cement mixer and the steering box from a Reliant Robin. This was a long way from the over-funded corporate world of modern-day motorsport. And I loved it all the more for that. A bloke in a shed who knew exactly what he was doing had put this thing together.

I pulled my crash helmet on, climbed in past the roll bars and was, once again, strapped down so tightly that my breath came in ragged gasps. I looked at my blue race gloves as my hands gripped the wheel. One more crazy roar up the runway, a piece to camera about the car, and then I would be back in the Honda heading for home.

Colin began the start procedure. I called for air and power and the engine began its slow spin. The noise built to the signature song of the jet engine as Colin stepped back and gave me the all-clear. With the power dial set to 125 per cent, I knew that this would be a full-power run and one I would enjoy. There was no fear of the unknown now.

Run starts: 17.30 and 16.89 seconds

I hit the button and release the brake. Inside the engine, a flame shoots through the middle of the spinning inferno and reaches the unburned fuel exiting out of the rear venturi. The already awesome power of the mighty jet engine is instantly doubled and it throws itself, the car and me forward.

Time lapsed: 14.25 secs; 288.3 mph

By the time my senses have sped up enough to keep pace with what is going on, I realise that something is wrong. This is not the usual push and pull of the steering as the front end scrabbles to keep the one-tonne car and its passenger heading in a straight line.

Time lapsed: 14.64 secs; 285.3 mph; cornering force 2.1 g

I am counter-steering now and battling something. My brain would later remember a sense of struggling to keep it going straight ahead, of having an elemental fight to keep on going despite something trying to throw me off course and into disaster.

Then I register that something terrible has happened and that I am in trouble. In reality, the front right tyre has suffered a catastrophic and total failure. The resulting blow-out registers on the telemetry at 273 mph and the car drops 100 mm before leaping into the air. On video footage, the front of the car leaps high enough with the explosion to lift the other front wheel clear off the ground.

Time lapsed: 15.00 secs; 279 mph; 3.9 g

I am losing the battle. The car veers off to the right. My steering inputs and corrections, assessed later by experts, have been well inside the speed of reaction expected of modern-day fighter pilots. The telemetry records show that I am inputting only the degree of steering required to correct the car's slewing path. My foot hits the brake – a futile gesture, instinctive but useless. I am not panicking, I am still fighting. But I am losing.

Time lapsed: 15.71 secs; 232 mph; deceleration 6 g

My last memory now. As the car veers to the right, I know that my steering efforts have not saved the situation. I am going to crash. I remember the parachute lever. I pull it. The car does not stop and begins to roll over. I register that it is off the road entirely now and is going to roll on to the roof. I can do no more. The next thing to happen, I am quietly convinced, is that I die. There can be no other outcome. I am not scared, my life does not flash before my eyes, there is just a calm resignation. And also a strange relief at finally knowing the answer to a question that perhaps haunts many of us: how will I die?

Well, at precisely 17.30 and 33.06 seconds on Wednesday, 20 September 2006 I believed I knew exactly how and when my life would end. And then I passed out as the g-forces generated by the crash exceeded those at which I could maintain consciousness.

Time lapsed: 16.17 secs

The car rolls upside down. The roll bars protect my head from the impact, but they dig into the grass. This acts as a ground anchor, slowing the car from 232 mph to 191 mph in just 0.46 seconds. My brain is thrown forward, hitting the front of my skull. The force my brain experiences overstretches some of the nerves and causes them to break. The resulting injuries could leave me paralysed, deaf, blind, or wipe out my personality, the person I recognise as me. But I am unconscious now and know nothing about it.

Part of the car touches down on the grass and digs in, sending the entire structure into another roll that turns into a flip. (Had I been conscious, I would have briefly seen a flash of blue sky before being plunged underground again as the car settled back on to its roof and began its final stop.) The avalanche of mud and stones kicked up by the roll bars ploughing into the field flips the helmet visor up, exposing my face. My left eye is damaged, the surrounding tissue pulverised. My mouth and nose fill with soil and mud as they are force-fed by the onslaught kicked up by the roll bar. As my head slews to the right, that side of the helmet is dented, cracked and caved in when it hits the crash structure. The right-hand side of my brain sustains more damage.

It ends just five seconds after the front right tyre blew. The car lies upside down. The wheels, exposed now to the sky, still turn as the engine cools. Inside, I am unconscious still, but changes are happening. My brain, thrown around inside my skull by the immense g-forces, is beginning to swell dangerously. My breathing is severely constricted by the soil in my mouth and nose. The arm-restraints have worked, keeping my limbs inside the relative safety of the cockpit, even upside down at 191 mph. The harnesses have done their job too, keeping me pinned in place despite the battering of the car rolling and pitching across the field. But I am in a critical state. As far as I am concerned, I have just met my own death.

Chapter 7

MINDY'S STORY

'OK, Ela, I'll be back in about an hour. Girls, be good and eat your tea and I'll be back before bathtime.'

I ran out to my Land Rover. Damn – I'd forgotten my riding hat. I threw open the heavy oak front door.

'Me again!'

Ela and Izzy laughed at me. Ela was standing with her arm outstretched, my riding hat in her hand.

Ela was our Polish au pair. She was with us during her break from university where she was studying physiotherapy. She'd arrived in June and had become such a friend. That summer we'd taught the children to swim in our tiny, previously frog-infested swimming pool. Every day after school the four of us – me, Ela, Izzy (our five-year-old) and Willow (three) – would run to the pool with boogie-box and towels and splash about until the sun disappeared.

Ela and I spent many nights in front of some great films which we would end up ignoring, gossiping instead as we sipped a naff bottle of wine. Ela always helped with the animals, putting the pony in her stable or – her favourite task – feeding the dogs (five) and cats (three), which she did every night. The children simply adored her for the games she played with them and the love and care she showed during that summer.

Riding hat in hand, I leapt into my nine-seater Land Rover, a G4 110 Defender long wheelbase, and in a glorious bright yellow – love that car! – and set off for the stables to see my fabulous new horse.

I felt dizzy with excitement. All my life I'd dreamt of owning a horse. Then a few years ago Richard bought me a horse for Christmas. She was amazing, but when I took a break from riding while she gave birth to a foal and weaned it, I lost my nerve. So I'd sold her, which left me completely devastated until a friend of mine suggested I look at a fantastic horse who she said would give me my confidence back. I'd ridden him twice before this day, and on the last visit had decided to buy him. Today was to be my first 'lesson' on him.

Thomas was the most incredible-looking horse I'd ever seen. He stood sixteen hands three inches, and was chestnut with a white blaze down his face and three white socks. Just one look at him and you knew he was special. I'm five feet one inch short and to even get on him was a bit of a performance as the saddle was about a foot above the top of my head, but once on board I knew I was on the very best.

I parked the car behind the equestrian college offices (my future horse was on loan to one of the lecturers there). Thomas occupied a large stable in a U-shaped courtyard lined by about fifteen boxes. As I walked through the five-bar gate into the yard, I could see him in the far corner. The sun was glinting off his coat. He was like an oil painting, the very definition of power and beauty at rest. I approached him across the yard and couldn't suppress my giddy schoolgirl grin.

It was about half past five and the sun was still warm on my back as I crossed the grassy island in the middle of the yard. There were students and horses all around, but I didn't really notice them as I reached up and stroked Thomas's soft white nose.

'Hello, my boy.'

Wow! What a moment – he was finally mine. This incredible creature of impeccable breeding belonged to me! I fastened my hat and struggled to get my gloves on quick enough.

'Mindy! Mindy! The phone, for you.'

'What?'

My mobile didn't work at the yard, so Ela had rung the equestrian college.

'Mindy, it's Richard. He's had an accident. You must ring Andy.'

'Oh God, no!'

I hit the ground running and headed for the car. Nothing seemed to happen quickly enough. It was one hundred yards to my car, but it felt like a mile. The key in the door seemed to miss the lock. It took three attempts. When eventually the door opened, I threw my hat off, leapt in the car, stabbed the key in the ignition, jammed it into reverse, and my foot was to the floor.

Phone! My mobile had no signal. Oh no! I was almost airborne driving over the speed humps on the way out of the college.

At last a signal reappeared on the mobile and with it voicemail, and missed calls from Andy Wilman. I called him immediately but the line was busy. He was trying to call me.

'Aarggh!' I yelled, tears streaming down my face. 'No! No! Please God, no!'

As I turned into the main road, the phone rang. It was Andy.

'Mind, Richard's had an accident.'

'You mean he's crashed? How bad is it?'

'Yeah. Look, it's OK, he's moving his arms and legs. They're taking him to hospital in Leeds.'

I let out a despairing cry. 'It's not OK, Andy. He's still got whiplash from the last one.'

Richard had suffered severe whiplash just six weeks before when a van he'd rolled during a stunt had bounced on landing. He'd been in incredible pain. I had absolutely no idea of the severity of this crash in comparison. It was only when Andy said, 'I'll meet you in Leeds,' that I knew it was serious. He was driving there from London. He hadn't been at the shoot.

My mind was in turmoil as I drove, tears blurring my vision. I remember focusing on a huge oak tree in the middle of a field. It looked peaceful and full of life – and it broke my heart. Perhaps my world, our world, was ended.

I snapped myself back to reality and phoned Richard's mum, Eileen. It seemed to take for ever for her to answer. 'Please let her be home,' I thought. 'Don't let her be out, not now.' I couldn't bear the thought of breaking this terrible news to her on her mobile, in the street, or at work. She and Alan, Richard's dad, both worked as charity consultants and were always busy. Thankfully, Eileen answered. She was her usual jolly self, but within seconds her world was changed too.

Her first thought was for her grandchildren. 'We'll come and stay with the girls,' she offered. Then Richard's dad volunteered to drive me to Leeds. But that would have meant waiting for him to drive three hours to Gloucestershire. I thanked them but said I just had to go, and they understood.

After hanging up, I burst into tears again, screamed, yelled, wiped my face – and called my mum.

'Oh darling, no!'

She'd been worried about Richard doing 'all these mad things' for a while. Poor Mum has had enough tragedy in her life to know how things can go wrong. Her own ten-year-old son was killed by a 'careless' driver. Tim was holding Mum's hand under the bus shelter in front of his school when the man ploughed into them. He was torn from Mum's grasp and slammed into a lamp-post. She witnessed the whole thing, and his last look across at her before he died. She's always said 'things just happen'. She's right.

She said everything I needed to hear. So calmly, so gently, with such love. Another flood of tears exploded. I had little time left. I had to get myself under control.

As I turned off to the lane, I phoned Katrina, our PA, a quick-witted, intelligent girl who helped with all the various logistical issues surrounding Richard's hectic work schedule. I knew she could be relied upon. I quickly told her what had happened and promised that I'd call again on my way to Leeds. She was upset, but instinctively knew I'd need her.

As I rounded the last corner, I pulled it together, knowing I had about three minutes to make myself look as normal as possible for the children. I ran upstairs, calling Ela as I went. She'd been waiting for me, keeping the girls occupied. She joined me in the bedroom as I threw a case on to the bed.

'I have to go to Leeds. I don't know what's happened. I don't know when I'll be back.'

Tears were running down my face as I threw ridiculous things into a suitcase. Ela watched me with silent tears running down her own cheeks.

'Oh, Mindy!'

She hugged me, and for a moment I slumped against her and wept. But there was no time for emotion, I had to get moving.

I had no idea what I was doing. What should I pack? Pants and socks; a dressing gown – in hospital you always need a dressing gown. It almost filled the small suitcase, but I didn't take it out. It was him. It was comfortable. He'd like it.

I shut the case and ran to my office. The computer was on. I sent a one-line email to Richard's agent:

Richard's had an accident. SERIOUS. I'm on my way to hospital. Call me.

I looked at my watch – six thirty! I must go!

Izzy and Willow were in the playroom.

'Girls! Girls!' I called, trying not to sound hurried.

They appeared in the hallway, both staring up at me with a look of curiosity and anticipation. I was sniffling, but smiling.

'Daddy's gone and bumped a car again.'

'Oh, not again!' said Izzy, rolling her eyes.

'Yes, I'm afraid so. And he's ripped some clothes, so I have to go and take him some new ones.'

'Oh, OK,' said Willow. 'He is silly.'

'Yes, darling, he is.'

We hugged. Willow was easy. She was just three. But Izzy looked at me. Really looked at me. Her eyes filled with tears and so did mine. I knelt down, cupped her tiny shoulders in my hands and looked her straight in the eyes.

'It'll be OK. It will. I love you. Come on, Iz.'

She nodded, thumb in her mouth, then threw her arms around me. 'I love you, Mummy.'

I gave that little girl such a hug as she stood on the dark wooden floor, her big brown eyes welling with tears, her brave face fighting them back. How often we would relive this moment I had no idea, and I will never know what went through her clever little head that day, but she knew something terrible had happened, and it had happened to her wonderful daddy.

It was time to leave. As I reached for the car keys I noticed Richard's spare mobile was on the table. I grabbed it, along with my spare one and all the chargers I could see. I dashed outside and realised my Land Rover would be too slow and too obvious. As a

motoring journalist, Richard regularly has cars on loan from manu-
facturers and a press car had arrived that day. I knew I was insured
to drive it in extreme circumstances, so I ran back in and swapped
over the keys.

The girls were on the front step, both a little too quiet. I ran over
and kissed them.

'See you soon. I'm sure I won't be long.'

'Will you be back tonight, Mummy?' asked Izzy.

'Well, maybe not tonight, but I'll let you know as soon as I can,
and I'll phone you to say goodnight at bedtime – OK, baby?'

'Oh, OK.'

Her lips were quivering yet she managed to smile. We both knew
she was being brave for her little sister's sake.

'Bye, Mummy,' said Willow, a bit confused by it all.

I had to turn away so they didn't see me crying. Then I ran to the
car. I trusted Ela. I knew she'd look after them. In the meantime I
had to get to Leeds. To Richard.

As I drove out of the gate the tears came again, but this time I took
hold. I had to focus. There was no point in crying – I'd just lose sight
of the road, and then where would we all be? I remember taking a
couple of deep breaths as I drove along, saying out loud, 'Come on.
Pull up, for God's sake.'

I shoved the earpiece in and phoned Katrina. I had to organise
things, make sure I'd sorted everything out.

'I've borrowed a press car. Can you call the manufacturer? Explain
what's happened. The pick-up address will need to be changed.'

Katrina told me one of the tabloids had already called Richard's
agent. They knew he'd crashed. How? I asked Katrina to check what
was happening with all the other papers – I knew Richard would
want me to keep control of the situation. He wrote for the *Daily
Mirror*; I must make sure they knew what was going on. He was

always adamant that, as his employer, the *Mirror* should be kept in the loop.

While I was talking with Katrina, the phone was beeping; it was Jeremy and Francie Clarkson. They were on their way to a dinner party. At this stage all of us were still oblivious to the severity of the crash. Francie was very sympathetic. She was one of the few people on the planet who could truly identify with what I was going through. 'It's what we all dread, your worst nightmare,' she said, Jeremy joining in on their hands-free phone. They insisted I call them if there was anything they could do. I remembered our holiday with them on the Isle of Man: the girls adored their children, and we had all really relaxed; Richard had even painted for the first time in years. During our brief stay he'd surprised Jeremy with a beautiful watercolour. I wondered whether he'd ever be able to paint again.

I snapped at myself to stop thinking like that. He'd had crashes in the past – plenty of them. He was the toughest man in the world. I'd get to the hospital and he'd be sitting up in bed with a few bumps and bruises and a sheepish look on his face, full of apologies. 'I'm sorry, I broke stuff . . .' And I'd give him a hug and a kiss and we'd carry on as usual.

Then, suddenly, reality hit. Katrina called back to tell me that every newspaper was following the story. The accident was big news. As I was talking to her, the BBC news came on the radio.

'*Top Gear* presenter Richard Hammond has had a serious crash in a jet car. The vehicle rolled and flipped at an airfield just outside York. He was transported by air ambulance to Leeds General Infirmary where he is in a critical condition.'

'Critical? *Critical*?!' No one had used that word to me. And it flipped! It bloody flipped! 'Oh no! No!' I yelled so hard I could see stars. Katrina thought I was going to crash. The images in my head were dreadful. I'd never seen the jet car, so the image in my head was of the *Bluebird* of the 1960s before it raced across the salt flats in Utah. I imagined it going tail-over-tip and then rolling at high speed. I felt sick as I pictured Richard stuck in that thing. I wondered what state he was in. I imagined so many scenarios all at once. Our house was up for sale. Well, maybe we would just have to stay there and change things. If he was paralysed, we'd have to put in ramps and have things altered for wheelchair access. I'd get him a really fast wheelchair. It'd be OK. If he couldn't talk, I'd get him a great computer. Anything can be dealt with, everything can be overcome. Just be alive. Just, please God, I beg you, please, please keep him alive for me.

All the while the phones I had rang constantly. I didn't answer them every time, I admit. There are certain friends you know you'll open up to. You'll crumble. I couldn't afford that luxury. Richard needed to see me looking positive and strong.

I don't recall much of that drive. Memory is such a bizarre thing. I know I spoke with Richard's parents several times, although I can't recall in detail what was said. I remember checking Richard's phone to get a number for his editor at the *Mirror*. They hadn't been in contact. I felt I had to call them. Richard would want me to. When I got through they were amazing. They hadn't phoned me out of respect. They just wanted to give us space. I was so moved. 'Richard's a mate,' were his editor's words. 'If there's anything, absolutely anything we can do, call us, won't you?'

That had to be the blackest night. I don't mean in terms of sadness or misery – although clearly it was a really dreadful journey – but I distinctly remember looking at the road in front of me, the sky all around, and it seemed blacker than black. All I could see were the lights of cars and lamp-posts. No scenery. No buildings. Just black. Nothing was important. Nothing worth seeing. Just objects to avoid and a path to follow. The slowest, longest path. The sat nav displayed an estimated arrival time and the number of miles left to travel. The miles just didn't seem to dwindle.

The bulletins on the radio repeated the news. I turned it off. I was shouting at the car in front to get out of my way. The traffic was slowing me up and Andy was calling periodically to see where I was. He was going to get there before me. I didn't want to stop for a second, but my bladder was fit to burst. I pulled over at the dodgiest services I've ever seen. As I pulled up, I noticed a group of rough-looking lads in hoodies. I parked the obviously very expensive car as close to the building as I could and jogged in the direction of the loos. The lights were out. Everything was closed except the public toilets in the far corner. At the door of the Ladies there was a small yellow plastic A-frame that read 'Cleaning in Progress'. Lights flickered within. It looked to me like a scene from a cheap disaster movie. As I hastened towards that door I said out loud, 'So, now I get mugged. Excellent.' But even if every last scruffy, mangy one of them had tried to tackle me, I'd have knocked the lot of them to the ground. It was one of those times when a kind of radiation of intent surrounds you.

When I returned to my car, I got in slowly and drove steadily away. They watched me go. My heart was beating hard. The second I was out of sight I put my foot down and breathed a sigh of relief as I rejoined the dark road. I still had a long way to go.

I'd tried to call the hospital but they were naturally cautious about giving details. I left them both my numbers while they checked out my details with the BBC. Trouble was, my phones were constantly busy. I stopped answering unless it was Andy or Richard's parents, because I was desperate to hear from the hospital. Then 'unknown' came on to the phone screen. I answered it, and a man's voice replied, 'I'm one of the duty nurses from A & E at Leeds.'

'Oh, oh, hello.'

My voice broke. I wanted to know about Richard, but at the same time I was frightened to death.

'Are you driving, love?'

'Yes, yes, I am. Can you tell me how he is?'

'Not while you're driving. Can you pull over somewhere?'

'No I can't. I'm on a motorway.'

'Well, can you see if you can find somewhere to stop and I'll call back in five minutes?'

'Oh God, OK.' My voice choked with tears.

I drove on, scanning the road ahead for a turning. I couldn't stop on the hard shoulder – that was dangerous. Richard had a thing about people doing that. I had to keep driving.

The voice called back three times, at which point I was close to a complete breakdown. They were worried I might have an accident if they gave me the news while I was driving. The fourth time, a woman called. I was screaming with frustration.

'Look, you'd better bloody well tell me or I'll crash anyway!'

'OK, love. Your husband's had a blow to the head and he's sustained a serious brain injury.'

Serious Brain Injury – three words you never imagine hearing in connection with someone you love. They echo through your soul. Hit you like a lead weight. An injury to the brain. Not the head, the brain. And serious. My thoughts were spinning around: flipped; crashed; critical; brain injury.

My husband, my Richard, broken? It just couldn't be true.

'Where are you, love?' the soft Leeds accent asked.

I had no idea. I'd just kept driving. For hours. The miles never ending. It was the longest drive of my life. I vaguely remembered seeing a road sign.

'Manchester, I think – is that right?'

'Oh, you won't be too much longer. We'll call you again in fifteen minutes and see where you are. You sure you're OK?'

'Yeah, I'll be fine.'

I was shaking and weeping. My funny, brave, beautiful, adorable husband was ahead of me. But maybe it wasn't him any more. Maybe it would never be him again. We'd cope. It would be fine. Whatever happened, we'd get through it.

'Enough now,' I remember saying out loud. Sniffing, I wiped my face and took a few huge gulps of air. I was getting close now, finally.

Andy called. 'Where are you?'

'About ten miles away.'

'Right, listen.' He spoke softly. 'There're a lot of TV crews and press here, so we need to get you in round the back, all right?'

'Yeah, OK.'

'Call me when you're a bit closer and I'll guide you in.'

I was pulling myself together those last ten miles. I wiped my face, blew my nose and pulled on my armour, ready for battle. It had to be good, that armour. I didn't know at the time, but it was to stay in place for many, many months.

As I turned the last corner to the back of the hospital and parked up, I remember thinking how bleak it looked. I sat in the car for a couple of minutes, then Andy came walking fast across the road towards the car. His appearance was shambolic as usual: baggy trousers and a grey T-shirt, dishevelled hair and a couple of days' beard growth on his chin. I gave him a half-smile as he hugged me.

'What a day, eh?' I said to him.

He was relieved. He genuinely thought I was going to get out of the car and belt him. But all I cared about was getting to Richard.

Andy was closely followed by a lady security guard. They were both on edge. We were in a side road and the press were all over the place. Andy wanted to smuggle me in quickly without anyone noticing.

Did Andy park the car or did the security guard? I can't remember. Someone drove the car away to park it in a safe place, and I was escorted into the hospital. I expected a shiny doorway with bright lights and lots of glass, but in front of me was a miserable-looking dark stone lump. I couldn't even see the door. I shuddered. I didn't like this place.

I don't remember how we got into the building, but inside it looked old. Then, as we walked, it grew brighter, newer. The floors changed from stone and woodblock to lino and tile. It looked more like a hospital.

I felt numb. Few words were said. The pace was hurried. We turned a corner to two rows of lifts facing each other. I couldn't really hear anything. It was like being underwater. A siren could've sounded next to me – I wouldn't have noticed. I was on autopilot. I had no idea how to get to him or even where he was, but I was close. Every turn, every step, brought me closer.

The lift stopped. We walked down a corridor. We stopped. Double doors. An intercom.

I could hear my heart beating in my ears. It was like walking on the moon; everything was in slow motion.

Ahead was another pair of doors. The lights were dimmed inside. A nurse standing next to the doors was smiling at me. Andy quietly disappeared.

The nurse said something. We walked. I saw a curtain drawn around a bed on my right. Was that him? No. We kept walking. Beeping noises. The sounds of machines. Intensive care. Past the curtains; the next bed. It was him. Banks of machines on either side; a ventilator pumping breath into his lungs; drips in both arms; monitors stuck to his chest and hand. His face yellowed with bruising; a bizarre lump the size of a fist on his forehead; his left eyelid four times its normal size and deep crimson. A ventilator tube was secured in his gaping mouth by a bandage wrapped around his head. He was still. Not a flicker of life. The only movement came from the ventilator as it deflated, then filled again.

I went to him, fought back the tears and kissed his cheek.

'Hello, my darling.'

The tears were dripping off my chin as I spoke, but I was half-smiling. Awful as it was, desperate as you may imagine it should have been, I knew he was there. I knew with every ounce of my being, he was there. Buried, tired, exhausted. But the spirit of this man who was as tough as any heroic warrior in a boys' storybook was dormant, not dead. I'd just have to wait for him.

Richard's nurse sat at the end of his bed, a desk in front of her like an enormous clipboard with records of all his tests and movements attached to it. She recorded everything regularly and plotted charts. Percentage of air in his blood; blood pressure; heart rate and 'obs' (observations). But mostly she just sat at the foot of his bed watching him. Watching the machines. Like some guardian angel with the power to reinstate life should it falter, there she sat – a warm, friendly woman with short blonde hair and a kind face. I instantly felt reassured by her presence. I trusted her.

I let my eyes examine Richard's face. I'd expected a real mess. Cuts, bruises, blood and gore. But there was none of that. As I looked now I could see how swollen his face was; it was that horrible yellow-green colour which you usually get around the edge of a good bruise. His left eye was really nasty. It seemed to swell more by the moment. There was a lot of dried blood around his nostrils, mixed with bits of earth. He looked exactly like Richard. But Richard himself I sensed was a very long way away. This was a husk, waiting for Richard's return.

It's very strange to live through a scene you've watched in TV

Grandad Leslie Dunsby on his bike in the 1930s.

BELOW: Nan Dunsby on her BSA with sidecar in the mid 1920s.

Grandad Leslie Dunsby (second from right) with his workmates at the Mulliner coachbuilding works in Birmingham in 1947. The rear of a razor-edge saloon is taking shape on the right.

Grandpa George Hammond in RAF uniform. He was in the Bomb Disposal Unit of the RAF. A calm (he would have to have been) and very brave man.

My father, aged about 5, ready to blast off on his turbo-charged tricycle.

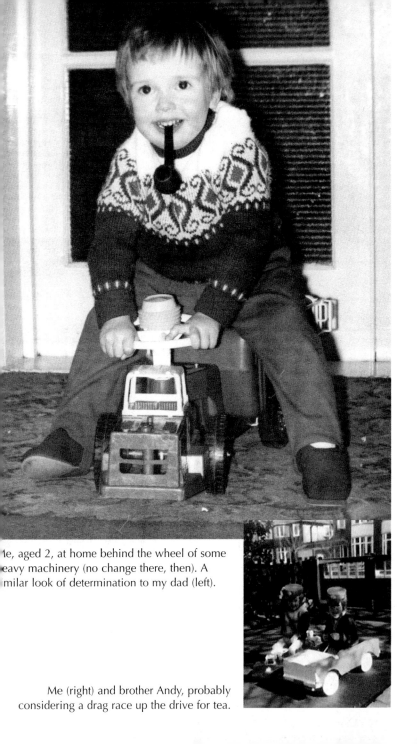

Me, aged 2, at home behind the wheel of some heavy machinery (no change there, then). A similar look of determination to my dad (left).

Me (right) and brother Andy, probably considering a drag race up the drive for tea.

Me, aged 3 1/2, and my first sports car – re-built by my Grandad, polished by me. I still love polishing them.

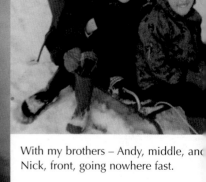

With my brothers – Andy, middle, and Nick, front, going nowhere fast.

LEFT: Aged 8, grinning for a school photograph. And yes, I was a little s_d!

In Army cadet uniform and in trouble too probably – judging by the discarded hammers I have just broken something.

BELOW: With my cousin, Martin, and my bike, setting off on a touring trip across the Midlands. I dreamed of bikes with engines.

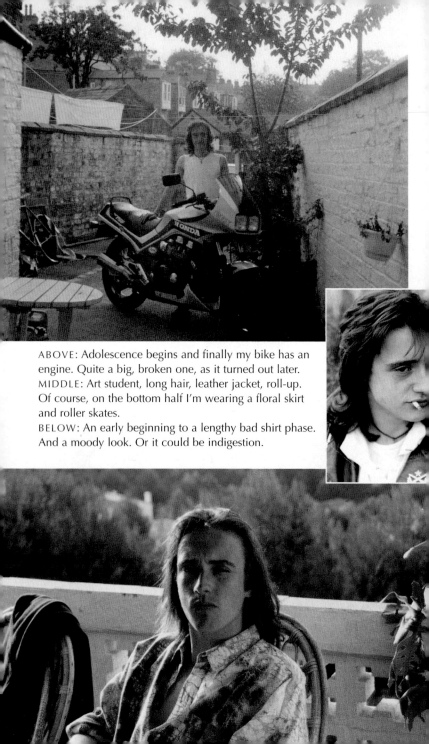

ABOVE: Adolescence begins and finally my bike has an engine. Quite a big, broken one, as it turned out later.
MIDDLE: Art student, long hair, leather jacket, roll-up. Of course, on the bottom half I'm wearing a floral skirt and roller skates.
BELOW: An early beginning to a lengthy bad shirt phase. And a moody look. Or it could be indigestion.

ABOVE: Camping in the Lake District with brother Nick. He's the one with a face full of Kendal Mint Cake, I'm sporting the enormous, bushy beard.
BELOW: Back to the Lakes, this time on the bike. The supermodel must have fallen off the back. Again.

Exposing white knobbly knees to breathtaking Lakeland scenery. Sometimes the picture you have in your head is not the one you are presenting to the world . . .

dramas so many times. There's a sense that the magnitude of this situation just can't be real; it simply doesn't compute.

So I sat there, holding his unresponsive hand – a hand you could squeeze, stroke, manipulate, but which gave not a millimetre of movement in return. There – but not there. It was awful.

The machines reminded me of my father in his last few days. He'd been diagnosed with cancer some years earlier. I've never been the 'nursing' type, but for the last three nights and two days of his life, I sat and took turns with Mum, until she was exhausted. Her sister, my aunt Betty, was there too. The three of us in his little room, watching him die. My sister Sarah found it all too much and felt she couldn't come to the hospital. She and Dad were extremely close, whereas I'd had a difficult relationship with my father until his last few years. As Dad's breathing became more laboured, Mum and Aunty Betty exchanged glances. It was eleven p.m.

'Oh no, Bert. Not today, not today,' Mum sobbed.

It was the anniversary of their son Tim's death.

'Come on, Bertie, just a bit longer,' said my aunt.

And he responded. He drew a monumental breath and restarted himself. He kept going till the following evening when, finally, my sister arrived.

She walked into his room and within moments of hearing her voice my father, who hadn't moved for days, lifted his head from the pillow, opened his eyes, smiled at each one of us in turn, dropped his head back on the pillow, and died. He had a look I had never seen before on his face when he died. One of pure wonder and joy. I smiled through my tears because wherever he went, he looked thrilled to be going there. But the thing is, he could hear. The whole time he was unconscious, he was aware of what was going on in the room. It is true what the doctors say in these situations: hearing still works. I was blindingly aware of that with Richard. Just because he wasn't giving any indication of being aware of anything going on around him, I was going to be as positive as possible. Just in case.

Every thirty minutes the nurse would carry out observations, asking Richard to do various things. Open his eyes was the first task. Then say his name. She would place her index fingers in each of his hands, and ask him to squeeze her fingers, then wiggle his toes. He did nothing. She'd be talking sternly and loudly at him. Still nothing. Then, 'I'm going to have to cause you a little bit of pain, Richard.'

She explained to me that she had to gauge response from him, and she'd use her penlight on a pressure point between his eyebrow and his nose, pushing and twisting the pen into it. It clearly hurt him, but his response was not great. He managed to flicker his eyes – little else. She'd hold open his eyelids and shine the light in each eye – he didn't flinch. He didn't speak. And when she tried to get him to squeeze her fingers, there was nothing. It wasn't encouraging. The reality of a life with someone who doesn't improve from this stage is frightening. How do you cope? I wouldn't allow myself to think about it. I had no doubt this was simply the beginning of recovery for Richard. I couldn't worry. He just needed time.

When the nurse showed me his chart and explained everything to me, I concentrated, digested the information, then filed it away until I might need it. I didn't want to know his chances. I knew him: he kicked, he fought. Because, by God, if anyone could heave himself through, it was Richard. And I'd be there when he made it back.

At the scene of the crash, when the paramedics reached him, they were surprised to find Richard breathing. The visor on his helmet had been pushed open and then filled with earth as his head ploughed into the ground. His mouth and nose were packed with soil and his eye was a mess. They removed as much mud from his mouth and nose as possible before using a measure called the

Glasgow Coma Scale to ascertain his condition. The GCS is scored between three and fifteen, three being the worst, and fifteen the best. Richard scored three.

Since the accident, we've spoken with the air ambulance crew who were on duty that day. I'll never forget what one member of the team told me: 'When you go to scenes like that, you can usually tell straight away whether or not they're going to survive.' I was expecting him to say, 'Oh, of course we knew he'd be OK.' Instead he told me, 'I didn't think he was going to make it.'

Once he regained consciousness, Richard stayed in the jet car while he was given verbal instructions on how to help the team get him out without causing further injury. According to those at the scene, he ignored everything the ambulance guys said, but when he heard a familiar voice, from a member of the film crew, he obeyed. They worked out that the only way he'd cooperate was if a member of the *Top Gear* crew repeated whatever instruction the air ambulance guys gave.

Head injury is strange. The impact isn't felt immediately, which was why, once out of the jet car, Richard made protests that he needed to do a piece to camera, but then became steadily more aggressive on his way to A & E. His brain was swelling.

At A & E he was completely anaesthetised to prevent him damaging his brain further. The drugs were soon switched off and their sedative effect ceased, but by then the effect of the brain injury had taken over. We would simply have to wait to see how he would recover, and what permanent damage there might be.

Richard had suffered most damage to the right frontal lobe. This is the part of the brain that deals with recognition, the ability to judge distances, decision-making, problem-solving and personality. He'd damaged nerve cells in his brain. The force of the accident had caused them to overstretch and break. These are injuries that aren't detected on CT scans, silent wounds that are extremely debilitating. Damage can range from paralysis, blindness or deafness to depression, anger or seizures.

We were told that he might never be the person he was before the crash. Some people no longer recognise their loved ones, or decide to change their whole way of life after such injuries, and simply abandon their family, their own personality changed for ever.

The future was, at the very best, uncertain.

Chapter 8

LEEDS GENERAL INFIRMARY

Memories of that night, and in fact the next couple of days, are very confused. Perhaps it's shock. So many horrible experiences in such a short space of time.

I soon understood that when one of the machines went berserk and an alarm sounded, it was because the monitor had fallen off Richard's finger. I grew accustomed to the routine. My husband was lying next to me on life support, still connected to all those machines, and as far as I was concerned this was my foreseeable future. I'd accepted it because to be unaccepting is madness and to panic is pointless.

Richard's younger brother Nick arrived at about 1.30 a.m. It was so good to see him. He had driven from Tunbridge Wells. He'd left his wife and his two young daughters and jumped straight into the car. Years ago, long before he was married, when Richard and I had been together just a few months, he was the first member of the family I was introduced to. I'd been surprised how little he resembled his brother. Nick was tall and slim with blond hair and sensible clothes. I worried he might be a bit stuffy, but as the afternoon passed into the evening I remember us all sitting on the floor drinking wine, Nick with my collie's head on his lap as he told hysterical stories and recounted daft rhymes. Richard, Nick and I laughed till our sides ached. He could recall every rugby song he'd ever heard, and his repertoire was astounding. He and Richard had spent many years on penniless walking holidays in the Lake District. They'd irritated and annoyed each other, got drunk together and shared good and bad times. I quickly understood why Richard thought so fondly of him.

Nick now worked in the City, his free time as rare as Richard's. We used to joke about his 'very grown-up' job in banking and Richard would make fun of him, often calling him on his mobile in the middle of the day in the hope that Nick would be in an important meeting and be embarrassed by his brother's X-rated conversation.

We hadn't seen each other for a while. His face was pale, but he kept calm as he hugged me and I explained what was going on. Nick digested the news. I can't imagine how it must've felt for him. They were very close and had grown up being daredevils and pranksters. Suddenly there was no fun. Just fear.

We sat briefly with Richard before he peeled me away. We checked with the nurse when the next obs would be and went downstairs. Leaving Richard was difficult. If he moved and I missed it, I'd feel dreadful. But I also needed to get a change of scenery, and Nick was good company. He was amazing. He was very upset, but dealt with it by getting on with the practicalities. He made phone calls, spoke with everyone and was a kind of central liaison from the moment he arrived. I've no idea how many calls he made, but he ensured that everyone was kept up-to-date with Richard's progress.

He'd bought a packet of cigarettes on the way down. We stood in a back courtyard to smoke. I've no idea what we talked about. I remember the cigarette tasted vile but I still smoked it. I suppose I needed that crutch.

At about 4.30 a.m., Richard's other brother, Andy, arrived with his wife, Andrea. They'd driven from Devon and by the time they arrived they were exhausted. I remember they were surprised at the absence of really severe external injuries when they first saw Richard. On a drive such as theirs, the imagination has time to run wild and I'm sure they'd expected to see him in a far more broken state. Andy and Andrea spent an hour or so with Richard before leaving to get some rest at a local hotel. They'd return in the morning.

Richard's uncle Brian, a retired businessman who lives in Harrogate, came to see his nephew briefly so that he could report back to Richard's parents. They were all those miles away in Gloucestershire and I'm sure Brian was there to act as their eyes.

During the night, both James May and Jeremy Clarkson drove from London to Leeds. Jeremy had received a call while out at dinner explaining that Richard's condition had become extremely serious. Life-threatening. He got up from the table and said he just had to leave for Leeds. Francie, his wife, was worried that he might be in the way, and pleaded with him that there was nothing he could do. He'd said, 'I want to be there for Mindy.' And he was.

James heard about the accident on the radio, then turned on the TV and heard it again in disbelief. He got into his car straight away too.

Brian Klein, the studio director on *Top Gear*, was in a restaurant having dinner when his daughter phoned him to tell him about the accident. Brian, one of the most lovable men I've ever met, left the table, walked to the nearest station and waited for a train to Leeds. Elaine Bedell, to whom the *Top Gear* team reported at the BBC, was already at the hospital. She'd been close on Andy's heels.

As I walked into the reception area of the hospital, near the café, I could see the whole gang had taken over a corner. They were all looking at the morning papers. It was ridiculous. Richard's crash was front-page news everywhere, and the TV stations had been showing bulletins through the night. At our home in Gloucestershire, the press had been into the local pub. They'd received no help from the locals at all, but had soon discovered where we lived, and started camping outside.

I remember vividly the first time the nurse caused Richard some pain and he reacted. It was terrifying. His arms flailing wildly, he tore off monitors and grabbed at the drips, all the while so disorientated he could scarcely lift his head from the pillow. But the tough, scrappy Richard was there, ready to fight his corner with every last ounce of strength. The episode was brief but explosive. When he'd calmed a little, the nurse did the obs and made notes. He was trying to respond to commands, but it wasn't good. He couldn't open his eyelids; couldn't speak. The nurse felt an almost undetectable movement with his right hand; his feet didn't move. It was like watching a child learn to walk. You concentrate on the slightest improvement, you will them to succeed. I sat there and silently prayed. I felt desperate.

The next time she did obs it was worse. Again, he didn't respond, so she caused him more pain. This time he managed to tear a drip out of his arm and almost hit the nurse in the face. It was so disturbing. He was out of control, quite literally; there was no coordination; his brain wasn't getting the messages right. And there was something else: as the nurse shone the light into his eyes, I saw for the first time the awful mess which was once his left eye. Beneath the lid there was no white, it was all red. Worse than that, the pupil wasn't recognisable – just a dark lumpy mass. What I saw burned into my soul. I drank in the image, wanted to cry, and then thought, 'It's just an eye. He's got another one. He can cope with one eye.'

He wasn't speaking. He just grunted. He was still very bad at squeezing the nurse's fingers. But what was really worrying was the lack of response from his left-hand side. There were small improvements with all of his other responses, but the left side of his body was essentially paralysed, and I'd already been told that the impact had been mostly to the right side of his head, controlling left-hand-side motor skills.

Every minute at his bedside was an eternity. Time was suspended in intensive care. I'd no idea if it was night or day, and didn't really want to know. My world was in front of me, in that bed with tubes and monitors all over him. But although it was soul destroying to be there, I was determined to be as upbeat as possible. After all, I knew Richard. If he thought he was missing out, he'd be more inclined to come back and join the party.

At one point his nurse came over and said, 'Has anyone told you what's going on in the bed next door?'

'Oh, um, no.'

She explained that the lad in the bed next to Richard's, with the curtain drawn, was dying. His family had been called in and he was going to die that night.

'How awful.'

I took hold of Richard's left hand and spent the next few hours listening to the terrible sounds you hear as a body slowly leaves this life. That 'rattle' in the throat, the breathing getting steadily weaker, and finally the sad exchanges between mourning relatives just feet away.

I looked at Richard's vacant face, a face I knew so well. Every inch familiar and wonderful but now inanimate. There I sat, listening to someone die just feet away, and willing my husband to stay alive.

It was obvious when the terrible moment came, and when it did something very strange happened. A cold chill brushed past me. It hovered as a ghost might, as if it were the spirit of the lad next door coming to have a look at Richard. It was suspended there for a second or two, then it left. I'd like to think he was joining with me, willing Richard to pull through; perhaps telling Richard it wasn't his time yet.

The nurses quietly asked all visitors to leave. When I returned, there was a fresh bed, and all the staff had moved on. It struck me then that death must be a common factor in their job. I wondered how they could be so upbeat when someone had just died, but I suppose that's the only way for them to do their job. They really are amazing people.

I resumed my post next to Richard. His monitors had quickly become familiar to me, and I was careful to position myself so that I didn't interfere with any of the tubes. I felt surplus to requirements. I'm usually so busy. I'd never been in such an alien situation. All I could do was sit and wait and pray. The hospital staff had warned us that the first forty-eight hours were vital; we'd know more about the damage to his brain after that. It's a little piece of knowledge you wish you hadn't been given, because while trying to be optimistic, a glint of stark reality is visible just around the corner.

His obs improved slightly. He managed to lift one of the fingers on his right hand. It was a breakthrough! The relief was overwhelming. A message had reached its destination from his brain at last. I remember thinking, 'Something worked! If one thing works, then so will another.'

The next few obs showed more slight improvement, as if he was on his way back. But then, at about four a.m., he started to dip badly. He just wasn't interested; he wasn't trying.

I looked at the nurse.

'It's bad, isn't it?'

'It's not good,' she admitted.

She'd tried causing him pain, but on this occasion it hadn't worked. For the first time I really felt I was going to lose him.

'Richard! Richard!' She was really shouting at him.

'Can I shout at him? The way I do when he's drunk?'

'Try anything, love.'

I looked around me at the other beds. There were three other patients in the ward.

'I'll probably wake everyone up, though.'

'That doesn't matter. You go ahead.'

The way she spoke confirmed she was as worried as I was. She had her index fingers inside his limp hands, but nothing was happening. Nothing.

I took a deep breath, got close to his face and yelled, 'Richard, you squeeze those fingers! Squeeze those bloody fingers! It's important!'

The tears were running down my face. Both the nurse and I were hunched over him, watching his hands, and as I finished yelling he made a very tiny movement with his fingers. Both middle fingers! The relief was so great! I half thought I'd pass out. The only time I ever shout at him is on rare occasions when he's been on a boozy night out with the boys and decided to sleep on the sofa. It's the only way to bring him round and get him to bed.

He has confided since that he remembers thinking he was tired, and there was a nice, easy route ... he could just drift away ... check out. That was what he'd decided to do. Check out. He said it was as though he was playing a game, but he remembers being jolted back. His mind suddenly recognised he was in trouble. He realised he'd upset me and he ought to stop playing the game. He was a naughty schoolboy who'd been reprimanded and had to pull himself back to face the music.

It is, I now believe, no coincidence that we refer to people 'pulling through', because that's precisely what Richard did. He pulled himself back. He has referred to the incredible determination and strength it took to 'pull himself back' at that moment. Remaining stationary meant certain death or disability. I'm so very grateful he made the effort, exhausted as he was.

Chapter 9

HE IS NOT GOING TO DIE

As I rang for the lift, I was thrilled and excited. When it arrived and the metal doors opened, Andy was facing me. His face was ashen.

I smiled. 'He moved both his hands.'

Andy burst into tears and threw his arms around me. He felt so responsible, but not only that, he loved Richard. They were mates.

Choking through his tears, he said, 'What am I doing? I'm supposed to be supporting you, not the other way round!'

It didn't matter. Richard had responded. Something magical had happened.

I called home and Richard's mum answered. I told her the good news and she was thrilled. We caught up on Richard's progress, and chatted about the girls. Richard's mum agreed that the TV and radio should be off while the children were around. We couldn't be sure how his condition would be reported. We decided not to send them to school or nursery, for fear of miscommunication about Daddy's condition.

I had a quick chat with both Izzy and Willow. They asked if I was coming home. It was hard to be jolly with them, but I tried to explain that Daddy needed me for a bit longer, and I'd be home soon. Besides, they had Grandy and Poppa with them, and that was fun.

It was tough, talking to Izzy. She was so perceptive. She knew there was too much fuss being made. I'd gone away. I never left them like that, and she could see straight through the facade. Izzy knew I was keeping things from her, and we both knew she'd made her mind up to humour me. I told her how wonderful she was, then said, 'Be good for Grandy and Poppa.' But when we said goodbye her voice, previously light-hearted, suddenly faltered. I spoke with Ela briefly after that, and asked her to really watch over Izzy.

Richard's mum told me there were TV crews and reporters around the house. It was the first time we'd experienced big press attention. We lived quietly in our house in the valley. People knew where Richard lived, and the kids on the school bus craned their necks to try and spot him in the drive as they went past in the mornings, but nobody made a fuss. Sadly, it was Richard's parents who were having to deal with it all, and this was an even more alien world to them. It wasn't as though the press were there to be difficult; they were simply reporting a story, doing their job. But for the parents of a man lying in hospital, bravely taking responsibility for his children, this was an added pressure which was hard to bear.

I called my mum to let her know that Richard had improved. She told me how she'd watched TV and listened to reports through the night. She wanted me to get some sleep.

'I couldn't, Mum. I'm not tired. Besides, I have to be there when he opens his eyes.'

'Of course you do. Try and get an easy chair or something to doze in next to him, will you?'

'I will. Thanks, Mum. I love you.'

Mum was desperate to help in any way she could. She'd offered to join Richard's parents at our house to help with the girls, but dear Mum doesn't drive and she's in her mid seventies. The turmoil of a normal visit to our house with kids, dogs and lunacy is often exhausting for her, and she was already taking blood-pressure tablets. She understood her role as support at the end of the phone was vital and I needed her to be there for me. I wanted my mum as much as my girls wanted me.

As I approached Richard's bedside someone from the hospital administration was waiting for me. She'd felt it would be difficult for the *Top Gear* team to have any privacy in the reception area of the hospital and had volunteered the use of a boardroom in the old wing of the hospital for everyone to use as a meeting place. She was eager to show me. So, reluctantly, I left Richard and accompanied her on the long walk to the old hospital.

It was all I could do to try to memorise the route. I'm sure people who work in hospitals forget that every floor looks the same. I was really concerned. I felt completely lost. It was as if a piece of elastic connected me to Richard's bed, and with each step it was being pulled to breaking point. The separation was almost physically painful, yet I felt powerless. This poor woman with her animated gestures and upbeat approach was unknowingly torturing me. I was accompanying her of my own free will, yet all I wanted to do was allow the elastic to pull me back. I seemed to be miles away from Richard. I hated it.

Eventually we reached the room. I vaguely remember walking in. It was unusually quiet, with people sitting around facing a coffee table which was buried beneath an array of paper coffee cups in various stages of consumption. Andy was trying to sort out sending a BBC press woman to our home in Gloucestershire. Jeremy and James were there, along with the majority of the *Top Gear* crew.

I said my hellos and sat down. It was so strange. I was trying to smile and be positive as I told them about Richard and answered their questions. Everyone wanted to see him, particularly Jeremy and James. Apart from anything else, they're all very good mates.

The newspapers were strewn around. Richard's crash was front-page news. I didn't want to see the pictures of the jet car. Yet somehow I had to look.

I couldn't stay for long though. I wanted to be back with Richard. I hated being parted from him. It took every bit of composure I could muster to talk with them all, speak with the press officers, answer everyone's questions. As soon as I could, I was running back down the stone stairs from the meeting room, seeking out a route back to the new hospital. I followed the flow of people ahead of me who seemed to know where they were going, and was relieved to see a familiar tunnel connecting old to new. I ran down the tunnel and jogged past the reception area towards the lifts, towards Richard.

When I arrived back at the ward I suddenly started shaking quite violently. I practically fell against the wall. Everyone had been warning me that I needed to eat, that it would all catch up with me. It had. I resumed my seat next to Richard and a cup of sweet tea appeared next to me. I felt so ridiculous. There I was, surrounded by a roomful of needy patients in intensive care, and the nurses were diverting their attention to some daft tart who forgot to eat. Even with their ludicrous workloads, they were concerned about me. I suppose it's a kind of nursing instinct.

Richard was becoming a bit more responsive. He was grumbling, and really making an effort with his fingers and toes. The worst problem was untangling him whenever he moved. There were so many drips, tubes and monitors, and he'd heave himself about without any idea of the knots he was tying himself into.

At eight a.m., Richard's nurse handed over to her replacement, Jim. It was difficult watching her go. I felt apprehensive about this new nurse. We didn't get off on a very good footing when he criticised me for putting the oxygen monitor back on Richard's finger when it dropped off. He was an older guy with glasses and slightly greying hair. He was very forthright and I instantly had the impression he'd stand no nonsense. His first obs with Richard were the most awful yet. Richard wasn't responding too well, so Jim did the 'I'm going to have to cause you pain' line.

'Oh, please don't,' I begged. 'He hates it.'

Within seconds of the pain registering, Richard was thrashing about. He threw himself into a sitting position and two other male nurses came running over. Richard grabbed the ventilator tube with his right hand and started yanking it from his lungs. He was gagging and fighting off the two male nurses as he kept pulling the inch-diameter tube from his throat. The two nurses desperately tried to restrain him. I was on my feet, tears running down my face, crying, 'No, Richard, no!' But his instincts had taken over. There was a tube in him which he wanted out. No one was going to hold him.

Jim shouted to the other nurses, 'Let him go! He'll hurt himself more if you try to stop him.'

They let go, and Richard gagged like an animal regurgitating food. But each time he retched, he yanked another few inches of tube out of his mouth. It was so frightening. I felt as though I was watching my husband commit suicide. The tube had been keeping his lungs functioning and he was rejecting it. I stood there with my hands over my mouth, completely horror-stricken. I looked from Richard to Jim, but there was nothing the nurse could do. That pipe took for ever to finally come free of Richard's mouth. It was about a foot long. Once out, he coughed and moaned, then collapsed back on to the bed and was out.

I asked Jim what would happen without the ventilator.

'We'll have to keep an eye on him and see if he can cope without it.'

I sat there for I don't know how long, watching the monitors like never before. I didn't want to leave him for a second. His breathing was very weak; his chest barely moved with each breath. But then, unexpectedly, his right arm started to move around under the bed-clothes.

Jim was beaming. 'That's what we want to see. He's checking his most important part is still there.'

'It's a good sign?'

'Oh yes.'

The consultant appeared with a neurosurgeon. They were studying his X-rays, and were concerned about an 'air pocket' in his jaw. They wanted to do another MRI scan to examine the spotting on his brain as his temperature had gone up slightly.

I didn't want him to go. The porters came to take him and I was told he'd be back in about forty minutes. But what if something happened in those forty minutes? What if he took a turn for the worse and I wasn't there? What if he woke up? It was awful, but I just had to accept it, calmly go downstairs and drink strong coffee until his return, all the while being chatty and positive with everyone who asked how he was.

Richard's obs weren't improving dramatically, but he'd try to open his eyes for Jim, and make very small movements with his toes as well as his fingers. Admittedly, the left side was still weaker, but it was responding slightly. Jim had called the optometrist to come and look at Richard's left eye. The consultant was concerned that it looked pretty nasty. At this stage the lid was practically all black with deep purple and red around the edge. It was so swollen it was almost impossible for Jim to open when he shone the light into Richard's eyes during obs.

Jim was different in character to the first nurse, but nevertheless a really good guy. He took what the doctors said with a pinch of salt sometimes; he'd been in the job for longer than many of them. When one of the young doctors suggested to him that one of Richard's drips could be removed, Jim acknowledged the advice. Then, after the doctor had left, he turned to me and said, 'I'm not going to do that. Bloomin' fool. And what? Put another one in the poor fellow tomorrow?' He was absolutely right too, as it turned out.

Trouble was, with Richard there was no telling how long anything would stay connected anyway. Later that morning, when he was brought out of his unconscious state, Richard decided to remove the catheter. It was another foreign body inserted where he didn't want it. He grabbed at the tube and gave it a tug.

'Richard, no! Don't!'

I tried to catch his hand, but he pushed me away. As he did so I realised his good eye was slightly open.

'Hello,' I said gently to him.

He looked straight at me, but there was absolutely no recognition whatsoever. His look was one of total disinterest. I wasn't even registering. It was devastating.

I walked to the toilets, closed the door, sat on the loo and cried. 'Where are you?' I was whispering as I held my head in my hands. 'Please come back, please.'

I could hear voices outside. I had to pull myself together, go downstairs – coffee, cigarette. I took a deep breath, wiped my face and walked out, staring at the floor till I reached the lifts. Everyone seemed to know who I was. Everyone stared.

The finger monitor which kept track of the percentage of air in Richard's blood was always the first to go. Whenever he achieved this, it set off the most irritating alarm. I'd become very good at re-attaching that one. The drips were what really scared me. The nurses were all so accustomed to dealing with everything, they were quite relaxed about the whole thing, but I'd learned early on that a broken needle is extremely dangerous; the last thing Richard needed was to break one of those in his arm. He proved pretty good at tugging them out, even with a ton of surgical tape securing each one to his arm.

Then there was the oxygen mask. This was a new addition following his dramatic rejection of the ventilator. He needed more oxygen so Jim and I spent most of the time chasing him around the bed trying to re-attach the mask. In the end, Jim decided that little tubes up his nostrils might work better. So he attached those. He was right, although we still had a battle to keep them on.

By this time, a great deal of positivity was building as Richard continued to make progress. He had started to move his limbs unprompted. Admittedly, it was either to grab a certain part of his anatomy or, his favourite pastime, to pick his nose. But it was fantastic progress. I should mention, in Richard's defence, that his nose was, at the time of the accident, completely filled with mud. Earth and blood caked together up your nostrils must be really uncomfortable, and his instinct was to try to remove it.

He hated doing obs now. He was really irritable about being forced to wake up a bit, but Jim was quite stern with him. Richard managed to move both hands and feet slightly and he even mumbled a couple of times.

I'd switched to Richard's right-hand side as he'd turned over, and was stroking his forehead gently when he mumbled something. I was so surprised, I nearly burst into tears.

'Sorry, darling?'

He repeated, and I just made out the word 'gearbox'.

I knew instantly what he was thinking about. Just a few days earlier something had gone wrong with my yellow Land Rover. I was sure it was the clutch; Richard had disagreed and said it was the gearbox. The local Land Rover dealer had taken it in for repair and told me what the problem was over the phone.

'It was the master cylinder,' I told him.

'Oh, OK.' He went back to sleep.

I was grinning like a Cheshire Cat. Tears rolling down my face. The box of tissues I had next to me was almost empty so I used my sleeves. It didn't matter. Nothing in the world mattered except him. He'd spoken. He'd remembered a piece of life, recalling his world – our world.

Less than an hour passed, and he spoke again.

'Where's the car?'

His eyes were still shut and I knew he was only semi-conscious, but again he was interacting and recalling things which were prominent in his daily life.

'What car?' I asked.

'The Morgan.'

'It's in the garage.'

'Where?'

'At home.'

He smiled slightly, nodded, and was out.

I wanted to tell the world! It was amazing! We'd had a conversation! But it was so heartbreakingly brief. He had dropped back immediately afterwards. It must have been such a tremendous effort for him.

Sadly, his next obs showed just how exhausted he'd made himself. He didn't respond at all.

Chapter 10

HELLO, DARLING

I've no idea how the day passed, but I recall it was evening when James and Jeremy came to see him. They'd been waiting patiently downstairs for so long, and the nurses agreed that familiar voices might well help him. Andy came too. We all instinctively tried to be jolly, and Jeremy was doing his best to be his usual self. He sat next to Richard and told him he was a rubbish driver. He was acting as normal, and a corner of Richard's mouth flickered into a slight smile. Jeremy was elated. It encouraged the larking about to increase, and Andy, although in a really worried state, started to look slightly encouraged.

Everyone was tiring though.

I was in the waiting room in the outer corridor with Andy and Andrea trying to order some Chinese food when the door flew open and Jeremy burst in.

'Mindy, quick! He's awake! He's sitting up! C'mon!'

I ran down the corridor, Andy and Andrea close behind. Jeremy was visibly moved.

'It was amazing! He just opened his eyes!'

We dashed through the double doors, and there, incredibly, sitting on the side of his bed, his hair dishevelled, his face bruised and battered, was my wonderful husband. As I reached the bed, ecstatic but apprehensive, he looked straight at me, a great dopey grin on his face, his good eye half-open.

'Hello, baby.'

He knew me! Oh, thank God! Oh, and how I loved to see that look. That cheeky, naughty, lovable look I'd wondered if I'd ever see again. He resembled someone woken from deep sleep after consuming an awful lot of alcohol and winning a boxing match.

'Hello, darling.'

I was so thrilled to look him in the eye as I said it.

He wanted to have a pee. He was offered a bedpan, but he wanted to go properly. I took one elbow and a nurse took the other, a second nurse wheeling the drip as we headed towards the loo. Richard was surprised at his lack of coordination, but kept looking at me and grinning. ''Ello!' And then, a few moments later, ''Ello!'

I thought my face would explode, I was smiling so hard.

'Hello, you.'

It was like dealing with a drunk. We had to stay with him in the cubicle or he would have fallen, but he was very cross at the nurse being there, so she had to agree not to look.

We all shuffled back to his bed. He smiled at everyone, said a couple of words to Jeremy, said 'Hello, mate' to James, smiled and passed out.

Obviously, I phoned the world!

The others left, and I encouraged Jeremy to go home. Francie had to go away the next day and I knew he needed to drive back to Oxfordshire to look after the children, but he sat there, arms folded.

'Thanks, Jeremy, you've been brilliant. But shouldn't you be getting back?'

'I'm not going anywhere until you agree to get some sleep.'

'I'll be fine.'

'Well, so will I.' He crossed his legs defiantly.

I knew he'd sit there until I did something, so I agreed to sleep on the sofabed in one of the waiting rooms. The nurses made the bed up and I thanked Jeremy for being so supportive before he set off home.

The sofabed almost filled the room. Through the slatted window set high in the door I could see figures moving past – nurses and visitors, all there to support and encourage the handful of patients desperately ill in the room down the hall. I sat on the bed with my bottle of mineral water, checking I'd turned my phones off.

I felt so alone. I was accustomed to being by myself – Richard's work took him away from home a lot – but I always knew he was at the end of the phone if I needed him. He was a part of my world even when he wasn't physically nearby. This time the reverse was true. He was only fifty feet away, but he could've been on Mars. I missed his presence. I felt hollow.

I spent a couple of hours dozing in the room before I escaped back to the ward. Everyone was satisfied that I'd had some rest, so the nagging eased up.

Jim handed over to a new nurse at around 8 a.m., and, when doing the handover, he explained about Richard's condition, before thoroughly enjoying telling her, 'Estimated speed two hundred miles per hour.' Richard's obs were more encouraging now: his responses were incredibly improved.

She thought it would be a good idea to clean his teeth with a blue sponge, about an inch square, on the end of a plastic stick. She tried to get it into his mouth, but he clenched his teeth together.

'Shall I try?' I volunteered.

'Yes, of course, love.'

She handed me the strange sponge lollipop and I tried to get it into Richard's mouth.

'Come on, darling, open up.'

He parted his teeth slightly and I managed to wipe around his teeth for about a second or two.

'Gerroff,' he mumbled.

'I'm just cleaning your teeth,' I said softly.

He opened his eyes and gave me the most venomous look.

'Sod off!'

I smiled at his nurse but inside I was heartbroken. He didn't recognise me. He'd looked straight through me. He'd forgotten again.

The consultants came and hurried about. They looked at his scans: X-rays of his brain clipped on to a huge rectangular light fixed to the wall opposite his bed. They mumbled and discussed various points, then came over to chat with me. They were concerned that Richard seemed to be suffering discomfort in his back and had been worried there might be some additional damage, but on examining the X-rays, he seemed to be free of other injuries.

Given his improvement over the past twenty-four hours it was decided he could be moved to HDU (high-dependency unit) later that day. It was great news. At last I felt he was really making progress.

Since his big lavatory expedition, Richard had been very quiet. He'd occasionally open his eyes but with no recognition. While he was semi-conscious, the nurse thought it might be a good time to remove one of the catheters in his left hand. Everything attached to Richard had to be tied on or stuck down, and his drips were held on with very sticky surgical tape. His poor nurse was trying, very gently, to peel this off his hand as he slept. He seemed perfectly happy, until suddenly, eyes still closed, he snapped, 'Piss off!'

The nurse continued to hold his hand. 'I need to get the tape off, Richard,' she said softly, and tried again.

'Piss right off! Ow!'

He pulled his hand away, briefly opened his one eye and gave us both an evil glare. We looked at each other and pulled faces.

'He must be feeling better, then,' I said to the nurse with a smirk.

He was still cross when it came to the next set of obs. The nurse was trying to encourage Richard to squeeze her finger with the hand which had the catheter in.

'Ow,' he mumbled, his eyes firmly shut.

'Come on, Richard, squeeze my fingers.'

'No,' he replied stubbornly, and yanked the hand with the catheter away from her.

'I think that's sore,' I said.

The nurse agreed. 'Sorry, Richard, I won't touch it again.'

He wasn't interested. He pulled a face, eyes still closed, and rolled over to turn his back towards us. We set about untangling the drips, monitors, wires and tubes, which had become entwined around him.

I left Richard briefly while the nurses prepared him for the move to HDU. It was great to be leaving the intensive-care machines behind, and to see Richard after his wash and brush-up. He was all clean and lovely. The bed had been changed; there were new, crisp white sheets. He was ready to travel.

He must have come round for a couple of minutes because, although I was at the coffee machine at the time, when I returned his clean sheets were splattered with deep crimson, as were his chest, one of the nurses, and the wall opposite. He'd decided to see what would happen if he turned the funny little green screw embedded in the back of his hand. (It was blocking off the tube which accessed his vein.) I think we all found out what that thing did, quite memorably.

We arrived at HDU, me looking like a zombie and him my most recent victim. The nurse was apologising to all the staff for the shocking state of her patient.

I'd never been to a high-dependency ward before. That was really quite a shock. It seems to be the place they put all the really ill people who can cope without having a nurse each, as they do in intensive care. Richard's two closest neighbours were both breathing through holes in their throats; one poor chap had been there, bed-ridden, for eighteen months. I marvelled at his positive outlook. The nurses were far more bustling and chatty in this ward. You instantly sensed you were with a gang of people who really enjoyed their work, and one another's company.

Richard was quite bewildered by his journey. He said a couple of things to the nurse along the lines of 'I'm sorry, I've made a bit of a mess'. He looked at me regularly for reassurance. Although I'm not sure whether he knew who I was, I think something told him I was someone to trust – after all, I'd been there constantly – so I suppose he sought comfort in familiarity.

I'd already spoken to Richard's parents about coming to see him. The BBC had sent a car to our home to pick them up and bring them to Leeds, where they could stay in the same hotel as other members of the family. They'd set off that morning, leaving Ela with the girls. Andy and Andrea had left to fetch their children, but planned to return as soon as possible. Nick would leave later that day to fetch Amanda and his girls.

I seemed to spend the day going up and down stairs. There were lots of flowers, cards and letters arriving from well-wishers. It was overwhelming. So many flowers had arrived that I asked the hospital if they'd mind storing them all in a room.

When I returned to the ward on one occasion, the nurses were all of a kerfuffle. The sister bustled over to me.

'Just to let you know, we've locked this door.' She pointed to the door leading into Richard's bay. 'We're worried someone from the press might get in.'

'That's very kind, but I'm sure he'll be fine.' It was rather embarrassing, and I wasn't sure it was necessary.

Then she explained that hospital security had alerted them, and they now had a security guard positioned at the entrance to the ward.

The flowery plastic curtains around Richard's bed remained drawn at general visiting times to avoid too much attention; although, to be honest, anyone intent on finding his whereabouts wouldn't have had too much trouble, once they got through the entry system. Richard's bed was close to a window, and the staff were concerned that photographers might manage to get a shot of him in bed, so they closed the curtains, but this meant inflicting misery on others in the ward who were deprived of the view. I'm sure when you're bedridden the view becomes far more important than the portable TV which each patient was allocated. Once again, the joviality of the staff was ever present. Their positivity was a huge factor in the recovery of many patients, including Richard.

All this made me realise that Richard had suddenly become big news, and no one knew how he was doing. Fortunately, his consultant neurosurgeon, Stuart Ross, came by later that day and suggested he make a statement to the press on our behalf which would update everyone on Richard's condition. He discussed how he would put the facts across, and it was reassuring to chat with him about Richard's improvement. It seemed the medical team were all astounded by his progress.

Every time Richard became lucid we asked him if he knew where he was, or what had happened. He kind of understood that he was in Leeds, and when you asked him where, he'd respond with 'hospital', but he had no idea why he was in hospital. I explained that he'd had an accident.

'Oooh, really?' he said calmly, as if he was humouring me, and gave me a disbelieving look.

I told him about all the cards and flowers he'd received, but it didn't really register. He sat propped up against his pillows looking blankly at me.

'You crashed, darling,' I whispered.

'Did I?' He lifted his eyebrows and looked vaguely interested. 'Was it good?'

'Mmm, pretty impressive,' I told him.

'Oh.'

His attention was drawn to a passing nurse with a cup and saucer in her hand.

'Shall we have a cup of tea?' he asked with a smile.

'Yeah, let's have a cup of tea. I'll go and get it.'

He smiled again. 'Thank you.'

He was too polite. He was talking to me as he would to someone he didn't really know. The move had tired him. His expression was becoming very glazed.

When I returned with cups of tea I was concerned that Richard's parents would be arriving at any moment and hoping he'd manage to stay awake for their arrival. Andy Wilman had been in to assure me he was going to meet them at the door. He wanted Richard's mum and dad to get angry with him. He felt they were entitled to be angry with someone, and he was volunteering for the job. I chatted with Nick and we agreed that would be ridiculous. Nick would make sure he was there first. Andy had been to hell and back with the rest of us, and it wasn't as though he could be held responsible for Richard's accident, even if he felt it was his duty to take the blame.

When his parents arrived, Richard made every effort to be the person they most wanted to see. He was smiling, sitting up in bed and making jokes. It was a heart-warming picture for his mum and dad; although they must have been dreadfully worried, at least their son, although obviously injured, was conscious. Sadly, it was clear after three minutes or so that his memory of the present was gone. He'd repeat himself again and again. He'd ask his mum and dad, 'Did you drive here?' They'd explain that a driver had brought them. He'd take a sip of tea, then, 'So, how did you get here?' We'd go round in circles. It was something I'd become accustomed to, and I warned everyone who visited that it would probably happen. Provided you drove the conversation and spoke about past experiences, or big plans for the future, Richard could stay pretty well focused and appear to be completely recovered. As he did when the Director General of the BBC, Mark Thompson, sneaked in to see him.

Mark was attending a conference elsewhere in Leeds and felt he simply couldn't be in the same city without checking in on Richard. Andy was running about like a headless chicken to make sure everything went smoothly, and when the DG arrived we'd all been well prepared. Richard was sitting up in bed grinning, and he became so animated, discussing programming and future plans with Mark, it was almost embarrassing. I wanted to interrupt and say, 'I know you wouldn't think it, but he has got brain-damage. He's just giving you a performance – honestly!' Richard put on an incredible show, and as I walked him out, Mark commented on how amazing he was. I agreed, although secretly I was very worried about him.

When I arrived back at the ward, Richard was much quieter. He was having a little chat with his parents and suddenly looked exhausted. He fell asleep moments after they left.

I went downstairs, turned the phones on and spoke to everyone who needed news. I'd asked Ela if she'd accompany Izzy and Willow to Leeds on the Sunday. Izzy's birthday had just passed and we'd planned a big party at home that weekend. Instead we'd get all of Izzy's cousins together at the hotel and organise a birthday party there after she'd visited her daddy in hospital. Not quite what she'd expected for her sixth birthday, but at least this way she'd know her daddy was close by.

The nurses had decided to move Richard into a side-room as soon as one came available, and luckily that happened very quickly. It took several trips to assemble all his bits and pieces in the room, but it was by far a better solution.

Richard's visitors were many and frequent during his last hours in the main ward. At one point in the afternoon, just prior to the move, James May tumbled in and shuffled over to me.

'Erm, hello, sorry to disturb. Erm, a newspaper has been on to the BBC to say that Richard was banned from driving for three months earlier this year.' He looked confused. 'What should they say? He wasn't, was he?'

'No, he wasn't, and you can tell them from me what utter rubbish, and how dare they?'

James grinned. 'Ah, yes, good. I thought you might say something like that. I'll pass it on.'

At about four p.m. on Richard's first day in the little room, I was sitting on his bed talking to him when he said, 'This is very nice. You're very lovely.'

'Thank you,' I said.

'But I have to go now,' he said sheepishly.

'What do you mean?'

'I really have to go now. I've got to go back to my wife.'

That was a shocker!

'No, darling, I'm your wife.'

'No, you're lovely, but my wife's French.'

Do you know, just for a moment, a million thoughts went through my head. Has he been having an affair with a French woman? Is he a secret bigamist? I dismissed them quickly.

'Really, I am your wife.'

'But you can't be. I'm having too much fun with you. You're too lovely to be someone's wife.'

Phew.

'Well, aren't you the lucky one, then?'

I smiled and kissed him as he grinned like a cheeky schoolboy. Then I left the room briefly to fetch coffee while the nurses checked his obs.

Alex, one of the *Top Gear* researchers, had arrived upstairs with Andy. I came out into the corridor to talk to them.

'Alex is going to be your personal slave,' Andy said with a grin.

Alex was smiling too.

'Whatever you want, whatever you need, it's Alex's job to get it for you.'

I looked from Alex to Andy and back again.

'I can't do that,' I said.

'No, you can,' insisted Andy. 'He's got nothing to do now *Top Gear*'s stalled. He needs a job, and you're it.'

'Anything you want,' Alex agreed, smiling.

'Great.' I grinned. 'Pants.'

They both raised their eyebrows and laughed. But it was true. I desperately needed more knickers! Poor Alex was sent out with quite a list: knickers, bras, T-shirts, a pair of jeans, socks, shower gel and shampoo. He also had to buy Richard some clothes, as they'd gone walkabout at the airfield – apart from his cowboy boots. Alex stood there with a pen and pad as we went through a list of items and sizes. Poor Alex. He'd joined *Top Gear* as a researcher to work on exciting and glamorous film shoots, and wound up buying underwear for the presenter's wife! Alex is a great bloke. I'd spoken to him innumerable times on the phone about shoots and filming issues, but this was the first time we'd met, and here he was writing down my vital statistics.

We huddled together in a side doorway to avoid causing any disruption. The corridor along the side of the ward was a busy thoroughfare. There were always two or three nurses seated behind the desk at the middle section which faced the doors into the main ward. The traffic along the corridor was constant: beds being pushed to and fro; orderlies and doctors; patients and visitors; nurses, sometimes walking and joking, sometimes running to answer an emergency call, but always busy.

As we talked, I saw her for the first time. A sweet, elderly woman with a dreadful gash in the top of her head held together with staples. It looked as though someone had drawn a thick black-red curve across her head through the downy white hair. The enormous staples were reminiscent of a macabre horror story. I don't know what happened to her, but clearly it was a nasty injury, and it was so sad watching her shuffle up and down with the aid of a nurse, hunched over, her left arm outstretched and index finger and thumb rubbing together, all the while calling gently 'Puss, puss' and looking into every nook. I could only surmise that when she received the injury she'd been looking for her cat, so she continued to look for her cat. I imagined she was once very beautiful. I had an overwhelming urge to take her home and look after her. Lovely as I thought her to be, would I cope with Richard if his grip on reality became this deeply affected by his injuries? How much further would he improve?

The following day was very busy. With Richard suddenly conscious and talking, understandably everyone wanted to see him. His brothers, Andy and Nick, had returned with their families, and of course

The girl I fell in love with

Blowing up a life-sized replica of the House of Lords for ITV in *The Gunpowder Plot: Exploding the Legend*. Yes, this is work. Sort of.

Grasping the PM's knocker. We had tea. I didn't spill anything.

THIS PAGE: On stage – *Top Gear*.

OPPOSITE (clockwise from top left): With two old men; a typical filming day; driving the Championship-winning Renault F1 car in early 2007. I had to come back in after 5 laps to have the tyres re-heated. They didn't sign me up; with Andy Wilman, *Top Gear* Series Editor and Executive Producer – and brains; And tells me what he wants me to do in the stretch-limo stunt; watching two of the worst parkers in the country attempt to park my hand-built Morgan Roadster on my ITV *Five O'Clock Show*.

LIECHTENSTEIN

Elvington Airfield, 20 September 2006.

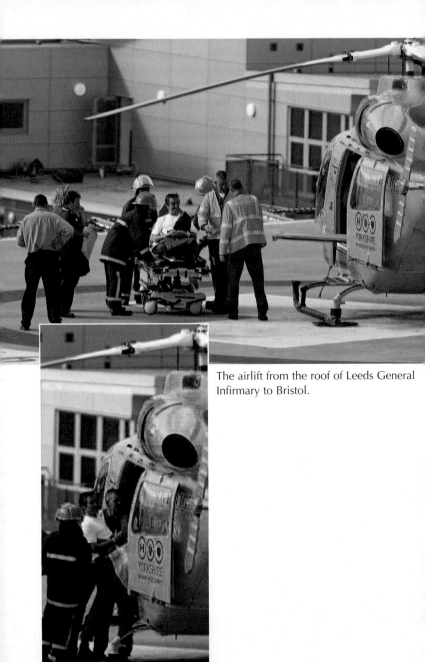

The airlift from the roof of Leeds General Infirmary to Bristol.

Richard's parents were there too. But there was a real problem. Richard was giving everyone who walked up to his bed an excellent rendition of the Richard he thought they'd like to see. He was acting the role of the perfect host – chatty, enquiring after their health and personal lives. Then he'd falter. He'd repeat himself, become confused, or most often take the conversation round in circles. I could see that he was getting more muddled as the day progressed.

I left him to deal with some matters the matron needed to clarify, and when I returned was horrified to find him on his knees, his hands cupped around the back of his head, his face buried into the pillows, rocking back and forth.

'Your head? Painful?'

'Yes! Oh God, help me! Aargh!'

I ran straight to the nurses' station.

'He's in pain. Really bad pain.'

Two nurses ran back to the room with me. It was dreadful. Richard was in such agony his face was unrecognisable. They fed some morphine into the catheter and I stayed with him until it took effect.

As he drifted off to sleep, the nurses could see how worried I was.

'Is the doctor coming round soon?' I asked the sister.

'Yes, they'll just be doing rounds now. Would you like a word?'

'Yes. Yes please.'

I sat down heavily in the chair next to Richard, watching as the expression on his face, which he was trying to shield with his hands, slowly changed. The pain and tension gradually dropped away as he drifted into a very welcome sleep.

It's strange how exhausting it is to watch someone you love in such misery. You go through every second with them, and you despise every uncomfortable moment, just willing it to be over.

When eventually he fell asleep I really thought I was going to be sick. I was shaking and needed to get some air. The nurses spent a disproportionate amount of their time encouraging me to leave Richard briefly. But they knew very well how difficult it was. Whenever he was awake, I wanted him to see a familiar face.

When he woke, the doctor came to see him. He asked Richard several questions and looked at his charts. He was very straightforward and businesslike and thanked Richard for his time. I followed him out of the room. He confirmed that Richard's condition had deteriorated, and suggested they reinstate the drip and keep him completely quiet for the foreseeable future. He'd been receiving far too much stimulus and from then on visits would be strictly monitored. He suggested I continue to be with Richard, but recommended only very close family be allowed visits, and then only for fifteen-minute periods.

Richard's determination to give everyone who visited him an enjoyable time had really taken its toll. Sadly, he was extremely good at acting, at kidding everyone he was OK. He could fool just about anyone.

One conversation we had over and over again worried me. It went like this.

Richard: 'Do you know what I'd really like to do?'

Me: 'No, what's that?'

Richard: 'I'd like you and me to go out there' – pointing to the window ledge – 'and sit together and have a beer and a cigarette.'

Me: 'We can't do that, Richard. This is a hospital and you're a patient. They don't allow smoking, and there's definitely no beer.'

Richard: 'Oh c'mon, you could get some, I know you could. And I've got some Marly Lights in my bag.'

He foraged in his camera bag.

Me: 'I can't get beer, it's a hospital. And you haven't got any cigarettes, honestly.'

Richard: 'Oh, but I was just thinking. Do you know what I'd really like to do?'

Me: 'No. What would you really like to do?'

Richard: 'I'd like you and me to go out on to that balcony and have a beer and a cigarette.'

Me: 'No, darling, we can't.'

Richard (checking through his bag): 'I know I've got a packet of Marlboro Lights in here somewhere.'

Me: 'They're gone, I'm afraid. Why don't I get you a cup of tea?'

Richard: 'Yeah, OK. I tell you what, why don't we take our tea on to the balcony and have a cigarette with it?'

Me: 'Because there aren't any cigarettes and there isn't a balcony.'

Richard: 'Yes there is. It's just out there, and I've got a new packet of Marlboros in my bag somewhere.'

He picked up his bag again.

Me: 'Richard. No balcony. No cigarettes. OK?'

Richard: 'Go and ask someone if we can just nip out for five minutes. Go on. Just for one cigarette.'

Me: 'I'll ask them when I get the tea.'

Whenever this conversation started I had to make sure it was brought to a satisfactory conclusion before I could leave him. Otherwise, left with the idea that the balcony was the ledge on the other side of the window, it could be dangerous to leave him. The other possibility was that he'd actually find some cigarettes and simply light up. He didn't have any, but I had some in my coat pocket. However, after the first of these conversations I made sure my cigarettes were hidden outside the room, and quickly decided to stop smoking, as the smell of cigarettes on me would just remind him of his own craving.

The cigarette conversation could take ten minutes or more to peter out, and it was regularly revisited with small alterations. The best one came in the middle of the afternoon.

Richard: 'I was just thinking; you know what would be really lovely?'

Me: 'No, what?'

Richard: 'If we could walk out of here, go out to the country and sit under a big tree, just you and me.'

Me: 'Mmm. That would be nice.'

In my head was a romantic picture of the two of us casually sitting up against the trunk of a large oak tree, smiling at each other through dappled sunshine, Richard in jeans with a casual shirt loose at the neck, me with a long skirt pulled up over my knees, laughing and smiling with tanned faces and windswept hair.

Richard: 'Mmm. We could have a nice cold bottle of white wine resting in a stream.'

Me: 'Oh, how lovely.'

Richard: 'Mmm, and a packet of Marlboro Lights.'

Nick had a similarly odd experience. I'd left him and Richard alone for a bit to catch up. Poor Nick had been so busy organising everything he'd spent very little time with his brother in any state of consciousness.

Richard asked him, 'So, what are you doing next week? I'll be in London. Why don't we go out for a beer and a curry?'

Nick responded, 'No, no, mate, you need to stay here for a while and get better. But we'll catch up soon, when you're a bit brighter.'

Richard: 'Oh, how long am I supposed to be in here?'

Nick: 'Well, they're not sure. Weeks, maybe months.'

Richard nodded. 'Wow, really?'

He looked around the room, seeming to be digesting the information, before looking back at Nick.

'So, next week. I'll be in London. D'you fancy meeting up for a beer?'

As you can imagine, with a severe head injury, balance is also affected. For Richard this meant enduring the indignity of my assistance every time he went to the loo. I had to become quite strict with him and insist I accompany him to the loo otherwise he'd fall over. This point was well proved one afternoon when Andy Hodgson – 'H', an old friend of Richard's from his radio days in the north – came to visit.

I'd left Richard in the care of H and Alan, Richard's dad. I remember as I left the room clearly saying, 'If he needs to go to the loo, go with him or he'll fall over. And make sure you take the drip. He forgets it's in his arm.'

'Yes, yes, don't worry, he'll be fine.'

When I returned to the room, they had left, but I noticed the remains of a broken drip on the table near the bed. Some weeks later, H related what had occurred.

He told me that initially, when in the room talking to Richard, he wondered just what all the fuss was about. He seemed completely normal. They were having quite a laugh – for the first five or six minutes. Then H realised that the conversation had turned full circle and started all over again, but for Richard it was all new. His short-term memory had completely gone.

I imagine it was very unnerving for H, but not half as difficult as stopping a grown man going for a pee on his own – even in hospital. As H described it to me, Richard swayed into the loo, shut the door, and seconds later there was a lot of banging and crashing and a little voice cried out, 'It's OK, I fell over, but I didn't pee on the floor.' At this point a couple of nurses came dashing into the room (he'd grabbed the alarm cord on his way down) and went in to rescue him. I suspect he had a sheepish smile and was giggling naughtily.

*

One of the loveliest memories of this time with Richard was the overwhelming happiness that he had come back. He was childlike and forgetful and difficult, but he was undeniably Richard, and I think I probably loved him more then than I'd ever imagined possible. A part of me knew he could've been lost for ever. Yet he'd returned.

Throughout this period the pain in Richard's head was still very intense and he was given morphine regularly, together with a cocktail of other drugs. The nurses were quick to tell me he'd be asleep all night. They were desperate for me to get some proper rest, and to be honest, I was really starting to feel awful. So at about 9.30 p.m. I left Richard and ordered a cab to take me to the hotel where the whole family were staying – visiting my room for the first time.

I joined Richard's parents for a bite to eat, and within about an hour Richard's brother Nick and his family arrived. We should've all been happy to see one another, exchanging jolly hellos and hugs, but of course this was no happy occasion. We were all worried, and there was only one place in the world I wanted to be: with Richard. Yet the mission was sleep, and I was soon on my way to bed.

I slept briefly and erratically, and by the time I turned my phone on at 6.30 a.m. I was dressed and ready to go. I was in the taxi when the hospital phoned. Richard had woken up and was distressed because he didn't know where I was. I told the nurse I was on my way. I was his anchor. Knowing he'd become so distressed that they'd felt it necessary to call me brought home to me how distraught he must have been. I would never sleep at the hotel again.

The taxi from the hotel seemed to take for ever. Although it was just a ten-minute journey, it was horrible. I was desperate. It's awful when control is taken away from you. I'm by no means a control freak, but I have, like anyone, a good idea of how fast I can drive, how quickly I can manoeuvre, and how much speedier the journey could be.

Within minutes, my phone rang again.

'Hi, Mindy, it's the ward again. Richard's getting quite agitated. I was just wondering when you might get here?'

'I'll be there in about five minutes,' I told the calm but obviously concerned voice. 'Please tell him I'm on my way.'

'I will, love, don't worry.'

But I did worry. I worried very much. To make him suffer any more than he was already suffering was just unforgivable. I felt as though I'd been completely selfish and stupid. How could I put him through this? Oh God! I was on the edge of my seat. Every traffic light was hell, and when I finally saw the entrance to the hospital I put my left hand on the door handle, the money for the driver clutched in my right hand. The second the car stopped, I was out like a flash, running before my feet hit the ground.

The two armed security guards on the door smiled and waved me through. I ran on to the lifts. Pressed the buttons on every one. Fidgeted as I waited. The second a door opened, I dashed in. I paced the lift like a caged animal on the way up. It was on floor seven. It took an eternity. I almost pushed the doors apart and ran like hell down the corridor, jabbing my finger on the button outside the ward door. They were clearly waiting for me as the door opened far too quickly. I half ran, half walked down past the nurses' station.

'Morning!' I said as I passed with an out-of-breath half-smile.

It was acknowledged brightly, with huge understanding.

'He's expecting you,' someone said.

'You don't say?' I smiled as I jogged past.

I gently opened the door to his room.

'Hello.'

Richard beamed at me. 'Oh, hello. I'm so glad you're back.'

We shared an enormous hug. It lasted longer than any embrace I've ever known. I wonder whether, as everything was so very confused and mixed up for him, perhaps Richard didn't believe I'd return. His memory was in such a dreadful state. Post-traumatic amnesia (PTA) is an alarming condition. For the majority of the time he had the memory of a goldfish (around five seconds). He could remember scraps of past history, just very little since the crash. I imagine he couldn't rely on his mind, which must be very frightening and confusing. He was described as being 'clinically confused'. The one thing he knew absolutely was that I was his ally. What he couldn't be sure of was whether I really existed or was simply a figment of his imagination.

I can only think he lived out a frighteningly realistic sci-fi nightmare where no one can be relied upon. You're told of an accident you supposedly lived through, yet by definition you should be dead. There are no serious injuries visible to support this 'crash', yet you have a chronically black eye and your head feels weird, as though you've been drugged. You vaguely recognise people, but you don't recall an awful lot of information about them, and you seem to be held prisoner in a small room with an en-suite bathroom. Oh, and lots of people turn up for some event that must be going on nearby to which you're not invited.

It's difficult to explain how our relationship emerged, and how scary the process was. It felt very much as though we were piecing together fragments of confused emotional memories. Richard was stumbling through feelings and emotions and trying all the while to understand how they related to us. He'd accepted that I was his wife (I think), and I regularly held his face in my hands and told him, 'If you have any questions, any worries, ask me. I'll tell you the truth.'

I'd heard so many conversations with other visitors who hadn't realised the importance of talking straight with him. He'd ask a question they considered stupid, so instead of setting him right, they made a joke out of it and answered in a flippant way. For instance, when he asked, 'Where's the party? Where's everyone going?' I once overheard someone answer, 'Oh, it's upstairs. We're all having a great time.' I'd immediately cut in, telling Richard there was no party. It was this sort of comment that compounded his confusion.

I spent so much time with him I was blindingly aware of the importance and credibility of every single word. I thought very carefully before answering his questions, and developed a huge amount of patience. But it's impossible to expect everyone who comes into contact with a person suffering from that type of injury to understand the complexities involved; particularly when, on the surface, the person they're talking to appears almost normal. He simply has a bit of a memory problem as far as they can see, and people act instinctively: if they speak to someone who appears coherent, they continue in their normal, everyday vein. It's only when the cracks show themselves as huge gullies that many of us will finally accept there really is something wrong. After all, it's far easier to believe everything is essentially OK than it is to accept that something has changed dramatically.

After that morning I didn't leave Richard's room unless he was either asleep or with someone. Whenever he slept and I left the room, I'd always leave him a large handwritten note taped to the TV screen, telling him where I'd gone and that I'd be back soon.

I would go downstairs and buy anything I could find at the shop that he might like – Curly Wurlys, Fry's Turkish Delight, fruit-and-nut bars, sweets and chocolates he'd always loved. James May had left him a copy of *Auto Trader*. Their favourite game was fantasy car-shopping garage. They'd each have a copy and select their favourite cars (unlimited budget) and pretend they could go out and buy them. It saddened me that, although I kept putting the magazine in front of him, he hadn't yet found his usual enthusiasm to go leafing through the pages.

There was a big hole in Richard Hammond, and I was very worried we'd never find all the pieces.

On my return from one of my trips to the hospital shop, I had quite a shock. When I opened the door to Richard's room, he was on the phone! The little wotsit had rummaged in his bag and found his mobile. I'd hidden the battery, but he'd taken the battery off my phone, which he'd found in my handbag (which he would never, ever have dreamed of dipping into before), and put it into his phone. He'd then – God help us! – called a newspaper.

As I walked in, he finished the call, blushed, and grinned at me.

'Who was that?' I tried to sound unconcerned.

'Oh, no one. Just a friend.'

'OK. Would you like to see what I've got?'

I showed him the contents of the bag and avoided the subject of the phone call. Soon afterwards, the nurses came in and gave him some medication. He quickly fell asleep.

The second he was snoring, I grabbed the phone. I told the nurses I was just popping downstairs, and when I reached reception I turned both phones on. My phone instantly rang. There was a message from Richard's editor at the *Mirror*. We'd been in regular contact since the crash, but now he was calling because, as he put it, 'I've just had a chat with Richard, and wanted to check it out with you before we go to print.' Richard had phoned him and chatted for some time – long enough for his editor to realise it wasn't quite right. After a brief chat he did the decent thing and agreed not to write anything, and he promised that should Richard call him again, it would be kept between us. Thank goodness for honest newspapermen!

I handed Richard's mobile phone in at the nurses' station.

'D'you think you could put this in a safe somewhere? Only, I just caught him calling a newspaper, and I think it might be best if he doesn't do that again.'

'Oh no! Yes, sure, we'll lock it away for you.'

I went to find Alex, our researcher/personal slave. He'd been shopping. He'd done very well, and handed over several carrier bags. When I returned to the room a sudden wave of panic crept over me. Where on earth could I hide the clothes? Richard was still hell-bent on escaping for a cigarette; I'd had to take his cowboy boots to the hotel as I'd twice caught him putting them on over his pyjama trousers. He was stirring as I closed the door behind me as quietly as I could.

I crept into the bathroom and shut the door. There was a mattress leaning against the wall opposite the shower that was to be my makeshift bed on the floor next to Richard. I decided to hide the bags behind that. I shoved them all behind it and quickly flushed the loo. As I walked back through the door, Richard was waking. He looked so unkempt. So lovable. His demeanour was one of someone just a little bit under the influence of a few sweet sherries. He was smiley and affectionate and very forgetful, but mostly he was still extremely tired. The nurses came in regularly to check his blood pressure, temperature, etc. and ask him questions. Did he know where he was? What day it was? What the date was? His name? By now, if they'd asked me those questions I'd've had difficulty answering, so I wondered how on earth he could be expected to remember. By the time they'd finished he was finding it difficult to stay awake.

I'd asked Ela to come to Leeds with the girls, and the BBC had kindly provided one of their drivers to fetch them, as Ela didn't drive. Alex came to the room to let me know they were getting close. I dashed downstairs to wait at a side door. I seemed to wait there for hours, although I'm sure it was only minutes. I'd missed the girls so badly.

When they arrived, I nearly burst into tears. I gave them huge cuddles, and then hugged Ela. Someone organised for the kids' bags to be taken on to the hotel, and I asked the lady in charge of administration if there was a quiet room I could take the girls into for a chat before we went upstairs. She showed us down one of the corridors along the original wing of the hospital. Finally, she opened the door to a large room with a boardroom table in the middle with probably twenty chairs around it. There she left us, Izzy, Willow, Ela and me. I picked up the girls and sat each of them on a chair facing me. I knelt in front of them.

'Now, you know where you are, don't you?'

Izzy, thumb in mouth: 'Yes, we're in a hospital.'

Willow nodded, straight-faced.

I hadn't really prepared myself for this at all, and suddenly I realised it was my responsibility to reassure and prepare these two little souls for something quite distressing. I hoped I could swing it.

'Remember when I had to dash off because I needed to bring Daddy some new clothes?'

'Yes, because he broke his ones and they were all dirty,' Willow replied, very seriously.

'That's right, poppet.' I smiled at them both. 'Well, when he tore his clothes he also banged his head a bit.'

Izzy pulled a face, nodded and asked, 'Was there blood?'

'Well, just a little bit, where he banged his eye.'

'Oh! Has he got a plaster?' asked Willow, excitedly.

'Sort of. More like a bandage.'

'Wow! That's really good.' She was impressed.

I looked again at Izzy. Her thumb was planted firmly in her mouth and her face was as serious as she could muster. I waited for a moment.

'Here's the thing. Because Daddy's banged his head, he doesn't really feel very well. He's really tired and a bit, well, a bit not like Daddy. But he'll get better. He just needs to get lots and lots of sleep, and then he'll be fine.'

'He probably needs a nap. He can have my dummy if he wants.' Dear Willow. 'I'll give him a big cuddle.'

'You do that. That'll make him feel much better.'

Izzy's eyes were looking watery.

'Did you make Daddy some cards?'

They were each gripping cards and paintings they'd made. Izzy had written him a letter too.

'Oh, you are clever girls.'

'Can we go and see him?' Izzy asked.

'Yes, in a moment.'

I had to explain a bit more about hospitals.

'You know that hospitals are where people come when they're poorly, don't you?'

They both nodded.

'Well, because the people here are so poorly, they need lots of peace and quiet, so you must always whisper when you go in. OK?'

They agreed.

'Right then. Let's go and visit your daddy.'

Ela helped me with the girls as we went upstairs. I'd already organised for the nurse to help Richard with his eyepatch before we came in. We'd explained to him that he should keep the piece of gauze over his eye as it looked quite gory and might scare the girls.

He was sitting on the bed when we entered the room. I'd prepped them just beforehand that we wouldn't be able to spend too much time with him, and they would be going to a party afterwards.

Richard was overjoyed when he saw them. But he'd completely forgotten why he had the eyepatch on and started trying to rip it off. 'Keep that on for a bit,' I gently pleaded with him, but he ignored me and tore it off. Thank God I'd prepared the girls.

'Oh, Daddy, that looks sore,' Willow commented.

Izzy was very quiet. She was assessing the situation. She spoke intensely with Richard about the card she'd made him. He was over-excited.

He got up from the bed. He was going to the loo. He hadn't managed to go to the loo unaided before this, but I understood that in front of the girls he would hate me to go with him. My mouth was dry as he shuffled into the bathroom. Before he was halfway through, he fell forward and saved himself by grabbing the light pull with one hand, and the emergency cord with the other. Two nurses appeared like a shot, and helped me to rescue him. We brought him back to the bed where he sat, grinning sheepishly. Izzy was very subdued. She tried to talk to him but he wasn't able to concentrate. The fall had exhausted him.

'Time to say goodbye,' I whispered to them.

Willow gave Richard a kiss. 'Bye bye, Daddy.'

Izzy's eyes really started to fill now. I looked at her with an encouraging smile and a nod, and mouthed, 'Say goodbye.'

'Bye, Daddy.'

Her voice was breaking, but he was half asleep, and didn't notice.

'Bye bye, darling,' he said.

His eyes shut, and I took Willow's hand, and lifted Izzy on to my hip. We walked out as quickly as we could to the waiting Ela. She picked up Willow as Izzy exploded into uncontrollable sobs and I hugged her to me, heading for the exit.

'Well done, Iz. Well done, baby. You're a very brave girl. I'm proud of you.'

Poor Izzy. Daddy really wasn't Daddy, and if ever there was a little girl who worshipped her father it was this one. But she was also very clever and very trusting. I put her down and knelt in front of her.

'Iz, he will get better. OK? He will. He's just tired.'

She nodded, and wiped her tears away with the back of her hand. 'OK, Mummy.' But I'm not sure she believed me.

'Hey! You've got a party to go to.'

Nick was waiting at the door with Amanda, who by now was cuddling Willow. 'Aren't you coming, Mummy?' Izzy was pleading.

'Well, I need to be here for Daddy.'

'Oh please, Mummy, please!'

'OK, I'll come a bit later. I'll come then.'

'Will you put us to bed? Will you be there for bedtime?'

'Yes, OK. I promise.'

It was really difficult, watching them walk away down the corridor. I wasn't quite sure how I'd manage to get away later, but it was important to the girls, and I'd promised. I couldn't let them down. Besides, I needed to be with them. No, I *ached* to be with them, to smell them, to play with them, to be their mummy again.

Richard was exhausted. When I checked on him he was very deeply asleep. It was one of those rare opportunities to get away for a few minutes. Straight away I wished I'd gone downstairs with the girls, but then that would've drawn attention to them, and so far they'd avoided being recognised. I wrote a note and taped it to the TV screen in front of Richard: *Gone for coffee. Back in 15 mins. Love you lots. Mindy x*

Seeing the girls had really knocked the wind out of me. Even though I'd comforted myself by talking to Ela regularly, and the kids every morning and evening, it wasn't the same. Seeing them was heartbreaking. I slumped against the wall of the huge metal lift as I went down to the ground floor.

Instead of grabbing a bottle of water or Coke from the shop, I bought a coffee from the snack bar and sat down with my phone in a quiet corner. Maybe I could make a couple of calls while I was there. I was just dialling a number when a woman tapped me on the shoulder.

'Excuse me, are you Mrs Hammond?'

'Yes, I am. Who are you?'

'I'm afraid I'm from the press.'

I couldn't believe it. The one time I had snatched a few moments for myself. To stop running around, to just be still for a moment and gather my thoughts.

'I'm sorry, I can't talk to you now.'

I scooped up my possessions, left the coffee on the table and half walked, half ran towards the safety of the lifts. As I went I glanced around, and suddenly realised how unusually full the reception area was. There were an awful lot of people sitting around with cups of coffee, and by the time I reached the lifts I understood why. The hospital was full of journalists.

I hurried back upstairs and went to the payphone near the lifts to call a few people.

The old lady was going for a walk with one of the nurses. She'd stopped calling her cat, but she'd obviously been trying to take her stitches out as she was wearing what looked like a pair of socks on her hands. I smiled at her as I passed, and she returned a weak smile. I'll never forget her face. I wondered where her family was, if she had visitors, if there were people at home who loved this dear, sweet soul. As I passed her, I whispered out loud, 'God bless you.' I truly meant it.

When I walked back into Richard's room he was just waking. His head was aching, and I went back outside to ask the nurses if he could have more painkillers. They'd ask him, 'Morphine or Paracetamol?' He was very good at avoiding the morphine, but as one of the nurses told him, 'There's no point in being brave. You don't need to be in pain. If it's bad, you can have the morphine, OK?' He asked for it straight away.

After he'd taken the pill, he looked about him, suddenly unnerved.

'Where are the girls? They were here, weren't they? I didn't dream it?'

'No, you didn't dream it. They were here. They've gone back to the hotel.'

'Let's go and see them.'

He made to get out of bed.

'You can't, darling, you have to stay here. Remember? You're in hospital. You had an accident.'

'Yes, but I'm fine. Come on. We'll sneak out. No one will know.'

He threw his legs over the side of the bed and I leapt across and grabbed the drip bag before he pulled it out of him.

'Where are my clothes?'

'You haven't got any. You have to stay here, darling. Shall I see what's on TV?'

'Oh yeah, OK.'

He turned his head and relaxed a little. I put the drip bag back on its pole, and hurried to switch the TV on.

Thirty seconds later . . .

Richard (sitting up and looking about the room): 'Where are the girls?'

Me: 'They had to go back to the hotel.'

Richard (horror-stricken): 'Who's with them?'

Me: 'Ela's with them. They're fine.'

Richard: 'Why don't we go and see them?'

Me: 'Darling, you have to stay here. You had an accident and you're still a bit wobbly.'

Richard: 'No one'll know. C'mon!'

He started to get up again.

Me: 'Darling, you really have to stay here. Shall I get a cup of tea?'

Richard: 'Mmm? Yes. That'd be nice.'

I was nervous about leaving him, and rushed to the tea urn. When I got back a few minutes later I couldn't believe what I saw: he'd found another mobile phone in his bag and was dismantling mine and putting the SIM card into the spare phone.

Me: 'What are you doing?'

Richard: 'My phone doesn't work so I'm just swapping the SIM card into this one.'

Me: 'Actually, I think that's my phone.'

Richard: 'No, I'm sure it's mine.'

He put his SIM card into the other phone and turned it on.

Richard: 'That's funny. Oh God, I think it is yours. Sorry, darling. Where's mine then?'

He started searching through his bag. I felt dreadful. His phone was in the safe, and I am probably the world's worst liar. The doctors had impressed upon me that he shouldn't be making calls and he particularly wasn't allowed even to think about anything work-related. That was difficult. The majority of Richard's friends were also involved in the industry – if not with *Top Gear*, then elsewhere. This was compounded by another problem: a great many journalists had Richard's mobile number, and he'd be only too happy to chat away with them, which could prove a bit tricky.

Me: 'Richard, you know you're not supposed to even turn the phone on in here, don't you? It messes with the monitors.'

Richard: 'Really? Oh, OK. You'd better turn yours off then.'

He handed my phone back to me and I reassembled it and

replaced the SIM card. He spied his tea and looked weary. His eyelids were heavy. His brow was knotted – headache again. The headache, he told me, didn't really ever leave; it was always there in varying degrees of severity. He looked miserable. He turned to me.

'Can we go home now?'

'No, darling, not yet. Not for a bit.'

'Come on, let's just go, they won't mind.'

I sat on the bed in front of him and looked him straight in the eyes.

'Richard, you've had an accident. You banged your head and you have to stay here until you're better.'

'Yes, yes. Now, let's go.'

I was debating what to say next when, fortunately, two nurses walked in. I explained to them that he wanted to leave. All the nurses knew I needed to get away to see the girls and at this rate there was no way I'd be able to leave him for fear he'd try to escape. They explained to him that he had to stay there, and for some reason he was more inclined to believe them.

The nurses asked him if he was in pain, and he was honest and asked for morphine. He really looked pretty dreadful. His whole demeanour was somehow deflated. He clearly wasn't convinced he'd had an accident, and seeing the girls had awakened all sorts of emotions. The nurses were concerned he hadn't been drinking enough water, and he'd eaten barely a thing. His drip was almost empty, and they decided to replace it to keep him going a while.

Shortly after they left the room, he asked me, 'Shall we have a cup of tea, then?'

'OK.'

I left the room with two empty cups. His memory was so awful he'd eat breakfast and immediately after finishing the last spoonful of cereal he'd ask, 'Shall we have breakfast now?' I never questioned him or corrected him. To do either would have been counter-productive. I went to fetch the tea, and when I walked back into his room, Richard had fallen asleep. Deeply asleep.

I poured the teas down the sink and wrote him a new note: *Gone to put the girls to bed. Back soon. Love you, M x*

I sneaked out of the room and stopped at the nurses' station before leaving the ward. I explained that I was going back to the hotel, but would return before eight p.m. They assured me I shouldn't worry. He was very tired and they didn't expect him to wake.

I sped across Leeds in a cab to the hotel and I was so thrilled to walk into a roomful of happy children. Andy, Andrea, Nick and Amanda, together with Richard's parents, had gone to great lengths to make a really special birthday party for Izzy. But although I gave the girls huge hugs and kisses and treasured each moment with them, my mind was constantly drifting back to that bed in the hospital. Knowing how quickly Richard would become distressed if I wasn't there when he woke, I was suppressing a rising sense of urgency. Although smiling and chatting with everyone, inside the seed of panic had been planted and was steadily growing.

The girls had been wonderful, but Willow was just three and very, very tired. Ela and I took Izzy and Willow to their room. I was so worried about Richard I was considering saying goodnight to them and dashing back to the hospital. But they begged me to stay and put them to bed. They hadn't seen me for two days, which was a first for them, and although they had Ela, I felt overwhelmed by their love and desperately sorry to watch them having to cope.

As I tucked them in, Izzy told me, 'I knew you'd come, Mummy. You said you would.'

I was so happy to hear those words. It's my code of conduct. If I make a promise to the girls, I always keep it.

I gave her a huge hug, and felt her tears on my shoulder. She didn't want Willow to know how upset she was, and I held her there for a little while.

'Well done, darling. You've a very brave girl. I'm proud of you.'

I went over to Willow's bed.

'Mummy, where are you sleeping?' No flies on Willow!

'I'm going to go back to keep Daddy company.'

'At hospital?'

'Don't worry. I've got a bed to put together in the room.'

Willow was cross. 'But, Mummy, we won't see you!'

'Yes, you will.'

Now she became tearful. 'No, cos you'll be there and we're here, so we won't.'

I made a deal with them.

'I promise I'll be back in the morning in time for breakfast, and we'll all have breakfast together. How about that?'

'Yeah! Yeah!'

'But you have to stay asleep all night and be good for Ela. OK?'

They agreed. I kissed them both, had a quick chat with Ela, and headed out of the hotel. I'd phoned for a taxi before bathing the kids, and knew it was waiting.

Leeds was very busy, and the journey took longer than normal. I was really starting to panic now. We drove up to the front doors, and I ran for it. By the time I reached the familiar corridor which led to Richard's room I was quite out of breath, but when I opened his door all my worries disappeared. He was just stirring.

The nurses came in and woke him for the usual tests and questions. He gave me some affectionate smiles, and when the nurses left the room we snuggled up on the bed and chatted for a while. By that time we were both tired. I helped him to the loo. He still had a hard time believing it was his bathroom next door. Convinced he was in a hotel, he would say, 'Don't go in there. It's someone else's room!'

His perception of time was completely bizarre too. After brushing his teeth and getting back into bed, he thought for a few moments and said, 'What're we having for lunch?' I'd grown used to his strange questions, so I simply told him it was bedtime. 'Really? Oh, OK.' He was very sleepy, and was soon fast asleep.

I dragged the mattress in from the bathroom and laid it on the floor beside his bed. The nurses had kindly left a neatly folded pile of bedding and a pillow for me. It was about nine p.m., and after switching off the lights I climbed into my bed and was soon asleep.

I woke to a most strange sensation. The hair near my ear felt uncomfortable. I rubbed it with my hand. It was sort of wet and a bit sticky. Still half awake, I was trying to work out what it was when something landed with a plop on my head. I rubbed it with my other hand and opened my eyes. As I focused in the dim glow of the nightlight, I noticed Richard's head over my side of the bed, his mouth against the safety rail, drool slowly leaving his mouth, trickling over the bar then dripping off and landing on me. 'Ooh, that's nice,' I remember thinking. It did make me smile though as I went to the bathroom to wash.

When I walked back into the room, I remember looking at him asleep and thinking, 'God, I love this man.' And in one of those brief, desperate moments, I whispered, 'Please God, help him.' I kissed his forehead and eased him away from the bars. I checked that his drip was still OK and made sure his arm couldn't get tangled up in the tube, kissed him again on the cheek, and watched a smile flicker across his face. Then I went back to my mattress. I knew I couldn't sleep too long. I needed to wake by five to get back to the hotel for the girls.

I tiptoed out of Richard's room at about 5.30 a.m. and told the nurses I was having breakfast with the girls and would (hopefully) be back before he woke up. They knew I had my mobile on me if there was an emergency.

I dashed to the hotel, having sent a text to Ela to check they were awake. I'd ordered breakfast for seven a.m. so we could have some time together. And we had a wonderful morning. To the girls this was more like an adventure. They'd stayed away from home, been to a party, and were having breakfast in their room. We tried not to talk about how poorly Daddy was, just how soon he'd get better and come home. Like most children, they were very persistent with their questions about Daddy's going-home date. I had to be vague. Nobody knew how long it would take, and I couldn't lie to them.

We were very silly and jolly during breakfast and Ela and I had a lovely chat. I couldn't thank her enough. She'd be returning home with the girls later that morning and we both knew it would be awfully difficult for them.

My phone rang. It was the hospital. Richard had called the nurse to ask where I was. 'He's a little agitated, so I thought I'd give you a call.'

'That's fine. I'm on my way. Tell him I'll be there in twenty minutes.'

The girls looked crestfallen.

'Oh, Mummy. You don't have to go again. Stay here with us. Please.'

Izzy was holding my arm and pulling me towards her on the sofa. 'I won't let you go. I won't.' She hugged my arm as I sat next to her. This was so unlike Izzy. She was usually quite independent, but this experience was unnerving her.

'Listen, Poppet, I need to go back and see Daddy because he's really not very well, and if I can help him to get better he can come home again, and that'd be good, wouldn't it?'

She gave a deep sigh, and the tears started.

'But I miss you, Mummy.'

'Oh, I miss you too, baby. So much.'

I gave her a big cuddle, and Willow ran over and joined in.

Holding them both was wonderful and dreadful at the same time. Leaving them was the most heart-wrenching experience, particularly when I knew they needed me. But this time Richard needed me more, and I explained to them very honestly why I had to stay at the hospital, and why they were needed at home – to look after the animals, and to make sure everything was ready for when Daddy came home. They sort of accepted this, and Willow began chatting about everything she'd do when she arrived home, but Izzy was quite reserved. Her thumb in her mouth, she simply nodded in agreement.

I had to leave. Time was ticking by. I told the girls to hurry and get dressed and they could come to the hospital and say goodbye to Daddy before they started their journey home.

I was all smiles and hugs as I left them. But once in the car I cried till I was halfway to the hospital.

Richard was sitting up in bed when I arrived. His face lit up. He was so excited about the girls coming to see him, but he was soon dozing again.

The girls came later with Ela. Willow held Richard's hand and looked earnestly into his eyes. She told him, very seriously, that he wasn't allowed to come home until his eye was better. OK? Izzy was desperately upset but very brave. She smiled at him and then hid behind me. When we left his room, she burst into tears in the corridor. I carried her to the visitors' room and once again told her how marvellous she'd been. Ela followed us with Willow, and when the two girls met up with each other, they stood silently and cuddled. They're very close, and each so supportive of the other. I was overwhelmed by them. They behaved amazingly, careful to remember everything I'd told them, right till the end.

We went down to the waiting car and Ela and I helped them into their seats. It was hard to let them go. With all my heart I wanted to go home with them. Still, I couldn't let them see me upset, so we chatted about how they must look after the animals and thank our neighbours, Anne and Syd, who'd been back and forth to make sure everything was OK. I promised them that as soon as I could come home, I would, and we'd talk all the time. I hugged and kissed them both, and Ela, who was looking after them so well. I told her to take them somewhere on the way home – wherever they wanted to go, to eat whatever they liked. I'd been to the cashpoint in the hospital and handed her an envelope full of cash. I had no idea when I'd be back, and she needed to buy food and supplies.

The second she saw the amount of money, she knew I wasn't planning on being home soon.

'Oh, Mindy, you're so brave,' she said to me as she hugged me goodbye.

'I'm not!' I whispered, but I hugged her close and swallowed my tears.

As the car doors closed, I remember smiling at the girls and saying, 'Be good for Ela, won't you? I love you.'

I stood and watched the car drive away until it disappeared. I wanted to drop to my knees and wail, but I knew by now Richard would be very fretful, and I had to get back to him. I took a deep breath, straightened my back and breathed out slowly. Then I began the journey back to the ward.

Chapter 11

A WAITING GAME

For the rest of the day, apart from Richard's brothers saying their farewells, I was the only visitor. Whenever he woke up, he asked the same questions every five minutes.

'Where are the children?' He'd no memory of them leaving.

'Where do we go tomorrow?' He was convinced we were in a hotel.

'When are you meeting up with the others?' He thought there was some kind of party going on, which was understandable, as it was pretty unusual for his entire family to be present at the same time unless it was a special occasion.

Other questions quickly followed: Where are my clothes? What time do we need to get to the restaurant? Then I'd explain (several times) that this wasn't a hotel, it was a hospital; there was no party; he couldn't get dressed because he had only pyjamas to wear; and no one was meeting at a restaurant. Eventually he would accept what I'd told him, only to become animated again a few moments later.

Where's Nick? Where's Andy? Where's Mum and Dad ? I need to speak to the *Mirror*. When are we filming?

The problem was, no sooner had you answered one question than it would be followed by another; then, seconds later, the first question would be asked again. It was quite exhausting, and sometimes very difficult.

The worst one was 'Where are my clothes?' He'd start looking around the room and I'd explain that his clothes had been cut off him at the scene of the accident, so he didn't have any. 'Are you sure? Have you looked?' was his standard reply. Once I'd satisfied his questioning on that one, his next move would be to grab his bag, or ask me to hand it to him. He'd start foraging through it, and I knew what for. It was the same every time. 'I really want to go for a beer and a fag. Let's just go outside and find a local restaurant/stare at the sea/sit by a stream and have a drink and a fag.'

When the sister appeared to check his blood pressure, I grabbed her and asked that she explain to Richard why he couldn't have a drink and a cigarette.

'The hospital is absolutely no smoking,' she said, 'anywhere on the grounds. And if you drank alcohol now you'd be at risk of fits and seizures. It's too dangerous.'

After she left the room, I spoke with him about why he was there.

'D'you know why you're here?'

'No, not really.'

'You had a crash, darling.'

'You keep saying that.'

'You still don't believe me, do you?'

'No, not really.'

Up to this point his memory of the crash hadn't seemed important. But sitting beside him on the bed, his eyes wide, seeking more information, I felt the time had arrived. Should I tell him, yet again, my version of what had happened ? No. It hadn't worked before so why would it work now? The TV? No – too dramatic. Get one of the nurses to come and tell him? No. By the time I brought them, he would've lost interest.

Then it came to me. The newspapers. More particularly, Jeremy Clarkson's piece in the previous day's edition of the *Sun*. He'd believe that, I was sure. It was written by Jezza, and there was a picture of the jet car, and Richard with Top Gear Dog.

Still, I wasn't sure if it was the right thing to do. I had no one to consult, and I must admit I was worried that he might react badly, but at some point he'd have to digest it, and at least we were in a controlled environment. So I reached down behind the curtain and retrieved the newspaper.

He sat propped up in bed, one knee bent under the covers. As I held the folded paper in my hand, our eyes met. I faltered.

'Are you sure you're ready for this?'

Why was I asking him? He had no idea. Was it better he didn't know? No, of course not; it couldn't be. He trusted me. I promised him I'd only tell the truth. This was the truth.

'It's a bloody big deal, Richard.'

I knew my eyes were filling as I looked at his face. His expression had changed. Suddenly he looked quite serious, and as he laid the paper on the bed, he was taken aback by the headline: *Hamster walks – and I watched, says Clarkson.*

'Bloody hell! On the front page?'

I watched as he read. I knew the article well, and was feeling every emotion with him as he went through the text. When he opened the paper to the double-page spread, his eyebrows lifted. He was really surprised. There was a picture of the jet car, and a huge picture of him and Top Gear Dog.

He looked at me, panic-stricken.

'TG! Where's TG?'

'It's OK. She's at home. You sent her home the night before.'

'Oh yeah. Thank God. When can we go home? I wish we were home now. Can't we just go?'

His attention had been broken.

'No, darling, you're in hospital and you have to stay here for a bit.'

'No, I can't. We've got to get ready. What time do we need to be at the restaurant?'

'We're not going to a restaurant, we're eating here.'

'But the others'll be waiting.'

He was getting out of bed.

'Where are my clothes?'

He was reaching for his bag, becoming quite determined. I knew we were about to get into the cigarette conversation yet again. My brain was desperately trying to come up with a change of subject, but he was racing ahead of me as he foraged through the pockets of his bag.

'Where are my fags? Someone must have a fag. 'mon, let's go to the bar.'

He was up and heading unsteadily for the door. I was close behind him.

'Richard, there's just a hospital corridor out there.' I spoke as gently as I could.

He looked at me as if I was some kind of fool.

'No, there isn't. This is a hotel. Let's nip out and ask Nick for a fag. Or Jezza. Who's next door?'

I wasn't going to stop him. What was the point? I hated trying to dissuade him all the time. He simply didn't understand why he couldn't join the party he firmly believed was going on without him. It was heartbreaking to watch him stumble the few steps to the door, intent on joining the others. In his mind, he was convinced he was ready to meet them and have a good time.

He opened the door and stopped dead in his tracks, the conviction of what lay beyond that door lost in an instant. He recoiled, and retreated. A glimpse through the door revealed the bustle of the ward: nurses rushing back and forth; buzzers sounding; patients wandering past. I caught him and helped him to sit back on the side of the bed. It was so cruel. I knelt in front of him as he sat and stared at the door.

Quietly, he said, 'Hell.'

I held his hands and kissed them.

'I'm sorry, Richard. I'm so sorry. It really is a hospital, you see?'

He nodded, but looked so very upset. I stood and hugged him. Not a romantic embrace. I held his head to my heart and kissed him through his hair. Wiping the tears so he wouldn't feel them drop. Feeling so desperately sorry for him. He was lost and I didn't know how to help him to find his way back. Perhaps he never would.

He tugged at the newspaper, which he'd sat on. It was still lying open on Jeremy's piece about the crash. He turned and looked at the article.

'Bloody hell!'

It was a big surprise all over again, and I was grateful for the distraction. He turned, the experience at the door instantly forgotten, and started to read.

For most of that day, the newspaper remained open on the bed. He read about the crash over and over. And each time the news came as a surprise. Eventually, when he took a nap, I removed the crumpled newspaper and stored it back behind the curtains. Whether anything would stick in his confused mind, I didn't know, but enough was enough.

We had some wonderful chats that night. We didn't talk about where everyone was, whether he was in a hotel, or any of the usual concerns. Several times Richard asked me where TG was, which I found really encouraging. Clearly, just seeing the picture in the newspaper had connected him with a small piece of new memory.

He didn't want me to sleep on the floor any more. He wanted me to lie with him. It was so wonderful to be 'us'. I had been frightened. There are many people who've been through a similar experience, watching as the person they love claws their way back to life. You watch and pray for the sparks of recognition, a flash of memory to bring the pieces back together so that what used to be can be rekindled, but there's no guarantee. We were lucky. We were strong before the accident, and in that tiny room with boxes of cards and gifts strewn around us, pictures of cars drawn by children wishing 'The Hamster' better, emails and letters from all over the world from well-wishers aged six to ninety-six, we fell in love all over again. My Richard remembered me. We were passionate and desperate for each other. Nothing else mattered. No one else existed.

We held each other all night, like our first time together. It was the start of the rest of our lives. He loved me without doubt. I hadn't once enquired how he felt about me. I'd felt he should make the discovery himself. Apart from explaining who I was and my feelings for him, there was never any reference to our relationship or life together. I knew it was quite possible he'd dismiss his life prior to the accident and wipe away all knowledge of our past. He could choose to love me or not. I wouldn't have wanted to influence his emotions in any way. Rather I faced a life without him than a life with him based on a lie.

Thankfully – and I am forever grateful – he fell in love with me all over again. Stronger, deeper, fuller. I knew then, whatever the future held, it embraced us together. We were one again.

The nurses knew that I was sharing Richard's bed, but no one minded. They never commented. All they cared about was the well-being of their patients. If having his wife with him made Richard feel better, then why not? I'm not sure whether we were unusual but I would imagine not. Anyone in my position would want to be with her husband, to help him with every fibre of her being.

I slept little, and was able to untangle his drip, catch him before he stumbled through the loo door, and prop him up from behind – both of us always half asleep. He'd changed from the private, slightly self-conscious man who hated me helping him to a smiling, affectionate husband who appreciated my help, enjoyed my presence, loved my love.

In the outside world, a storm was brewing over the future of *Top Gear*, with arguments for and against the series being cancelled. James and Jeremy, together with Andy Wilman, were adamant that the series was over if Richard wasn't able to return. In the media, some were vehemently opposed to the continuation of the show, accusing the BBC of being irresponsible and dangerous, and 'going too far'. Richard himself was starting to ask about the show. He was eager to get back to work, concerned they'd have to start filming for the next series.

Reports in the newspapers that Richard had been trying to set a land speed record were untrue, but I guess it was an understandable assumption. Jeremy was spending a great deal of time defending the programme, emphasising the significance of keeping Richard's job waiting for him.

Imagine. You've suffered brain-damage. You nearly died. You heroically fought your way back towards that huge goal, the first day back, and it doesn't matter, because no one's going to make the programme any more, and the job you loved, the programme you loved from childhood, has been abolished. And it's your fault. You killed it, because it didn't kill you. Had that been the outcome, had *Top Gear* been taken off air, I'm sure Richard's recovery would have been seriously affected. He would've felt guilty and miserable, and

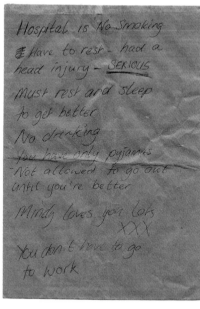

If you wake up —

I have gone to get a
sandwich.
Back in a mo.
Love you very much.

Mindy x

Hospital is No Smoking
Have to rest - had a
head injury — SERIOUS
Must rest and sleep
to get better
No drinking
You have only pyjamas
Not allowed to go out
until you're better

Mindy loves you lots
XXX

You don't have to go
to work

eeds General Infirmary: Notes taped to the
V screen by Mindy whenever she left my
edside and one of Izzy's cards.

To mummy and
Daddy I Love
You so muchand
when you come
home I'm going to
give you a big
cudle because I
Love you so much
I cant wait antill
you come home
home and Daddy
and me will clean the
cars and mummy will
help clean the cars to

Recovering in Scotland with some damage still visible to left eye

LEFT AND ABOVE: It felt good to be outside again. But a bit frightening

From the Health and Safety Investigation report:

'The immediate cause of the accident was a catastrophic failure of the Vampire's front offside tyre at 288 mph on the seventh high-speed run of the day. Examination of this tyre and video footage showed that the tyre was damaged, as a result of an object (or objects) having entered the sidewall immediately adjacent to the edge of the tread, during the latter part of the previous run. A blister was visible in the tyre's outside but this appears to have subsided and was not apparent immediately before the final run commenced.'

The telemetry results from the Racelogic VBOX show:

1. The speed of the car during the successful 314 mph run. It had reached 200 mph in less than 8 seconds. The fastest production car in the world, the Bugatti Veyron, takes 24 seconds to reach 200 mph.

2. The longitudinal G-force attained over the crash run – during acceleration a force of over 1.5 times my body weight was sticking me into the back of my seat. Once the tyre disintegrated, 15.5 seconds into the run, the deceleration G-force was pushing me forward at 5G, peaking at 7G – or roughly half a ton sitting on my back.

3. The crash run with the lateral G-force attained. Initially there is none, as the car is going in a straight line. After the tyre burst the car slews sideways exerting a G-force of over 3G, peaking at 5G. The most a Formula 1 driver feels in cornering is up to 4G.

etting back to what we call normal. Izzy, me, Captain, Mindy and Willow on
ard our MPV.

Home and Away: Izzy and Willow with Hattie and, below, back to work and the normal day-to-day grind resumes – racing Jeremy and James to the North Pole with a dog sled.

I daren't even imagine the depths to which his depression could've taken him.

Top Gear may seem a little gung-ho and dangerous, but it's very carefully put together, and the group of people who run around like headless chickens are some of the hardest-working people I've ever known. They're also intensely proud of the end product. Jeremy, James and Richard are mates; Andy refers to them as a band (himself included). When Richard was in intensive care, with James, Jeremy and Andy around him, I remember Andy turning away from the bed where Richard lay motionless.

'C'mon, mate,' he said in a broken voice. 'We can't go on without the drummer.'

The nurse from Occupational Therapy came and told us about post-traumatic amnesia, explaining the reasons for the daily questions by nurses to gauge whether Richard's memory was returning. Essentially, we were playing a waiting game. Every brain injury is unique. Every patient dictates his or her own recovery time. To remain positive was everything, so the nurse was careful not to voice what both she and I knew: there was no way of saying how well he would do, how much recovery would be achieved. He'd made amazing progress thus far, but brains are more complex than any of us truly understand. There are medical explanations for so many results, but talking with the neurosurgeons, it quickly becomes apparent that the complexity of the brain is phenomenal, and very frightening. No one can tell you if or when your loved one will recover.

The signs remained good though. To help Richard's memory we bought him a large A4 page-to-a-day diary. He was to write in there what he'd done, notes to himself, etc. When I needed to leave the room I could add notes to remind him of my whereabouts and when I'd return, always adding extra time in case I was delayed. His balance was slowly improving too. He could walk the few steps around his bed unaided while keeping his hand on the rail for support, and could manage a trip to the loo if he remembered to lean one hand against the wall. It was a joy to watch him take these small steps towards independence, sensing his frustration and then pride at each small victory.

But with strength came renewed determination. He was going completely stir crazy. He'd even resorted to watching a little television – a very rare occupation under normal circumstances. I remember one night watching *Who Wants to Be a Millionaire?* with him. The whole way through he answered the questions with great enthusiasm. I was astounded that his interest was held so long. He hated quiz shows, would never dream of watching one normally, yet he was completely absorbed. Then it came to me: he was exercising his brain, and to his great delight it was working well.

The flowers continued to arrive in overwhelming numbers. Only a few could fit into Richard's room, in particular a bouquet of lilies which made him sneeze – one of the most painful experiences for him post-crash. He'd hold his head and beg for painkillers. It heralded the end of flowers in his room, and from then on they were gathered together in rooms downstairs in the bowels of the hospital. I visited them with Richard's mum. It was a moving experience. I still have the cards from each bouquet. I took Polaroid photographs of them, as I knew Richard wouldn't be able to see them himself. They are images I will never forget, and the goodwill contained in those cards was incredible. There were balloons and soft toys, too, a great many from children. Richard had always said he was just a bloke on a car show. He was. He is. But the love and hope contained in those messages were for a bloke on a car show who was held in deep affection by a great many people. There were so many flowers they covered desks, chairs – everywhere. Their scent and colours overwhelmed the senses.

I was unsure what we should do with them, then Richard's mum had a wonderful idea. She asked one of the women, 'Do you have an old people's ward?'

'Yes, of course.'

'What d'you think, Mind? Shall we send them there?'

'That's a fantastic idea.'

A small army of porters descended upon the rooms where the flowers were being stored and set off with trolleys piled high. They were a glorious sight. Flowers went to as many departments as possible. Starting with the geriatric ward. It was a heart-warming spectacle. Wonderful to know, if you were one of those incredibly generous and thoughtful people who sent flowers to the little bloke from the car show: not only did you make a difference to his recovery, you also helped many others who appreciated the sentiment just as much. I heard from one of the matrons that the elderly patients were completely overwhelmed by the flowers when they arrived, and they brought smiles of appreciation throughout the hospital.

Richard's escape plans grew more complex. One night I found him trying to unhinge the bathroom window. There was only one sure-fire way to stop him: I hid his pyjama bottoms while he was asleep. Even in his confused state, he wouldn't venture out naked from the waist down.

After showering the following morning, he began searching for fresh pyjamas. He found the freshly laundered jacket, calmly buttoned it, then began looking about the room for the trousers.

'That's funny. No kecks!'

'Oh!' I called out nonchalantly. 'Maybe they forgot.'

I awaited his response, but there was none. He'd climbed back into bed and was calmly looking at the kids' drawings.

Andy Wilman had contacted the F1 neuro-doctor, Professor Syd Watkins, who'd designed the helmet Richard had worn in the jet car. Undoubtedly it had saved his life. He'd also dealt with precisely the same injuries Richard had sustained many times before with Formula One drivers. He had given Andy both his home and mobile numbers and suggested I call him if I had the opportunity.

When we spoke, he was reassuring. After asking me a handful of questions, he calmly told me the future looked bright. Richard was doing very well. He was convinced he'd make a full recovery. He also told me that many patients in these situations think only of one thing: escape and getting home. He recalled one man who'd managed to escape from the hospital. Syd had enquired whether any vehicles were missing. It transpired that, yes, an ambulance had gone. 'Go to his house,' Syd had told them. 'He'll be there.' They found the ambulance parked outside. Syd was right.

I couldn't risk Richard escaping. Knowing his determination and ingenuity, it would be the fastest car or bike in the car park he'd choose for his getaway, not an ambulance.

The nurses and doctors were concerned that a controlled environment was still essential, but Richard was desperate to escape the confines of his room. After a long chat at the nurses' station, we came up with a plan to get him out into the fresh air.

A porter came to his room pushing a wheelchair for his use, a security guard alongside. Richard (with pyjama bottoms now 'found') took his seat, grinning from ear to ear. He was laughing and very embarrassed at being forced to be a passenger, apologising to the porter, joking that he was being bullied by all these women, but scared they'd turn on him if he tried to get out. When he saw the security guard, his first words were, 'Oh, come on, is this really necessary?'

The security guard laughed. 'I'm afraid so.'

We were all getting quite giggly. Richard's excitement was contagious. The sister was coming with us, and she'd given Richard a pair of sunglasses and put a blanket over his head. By this time we really were close to collapse. Richard looked like a criminal about to be bundled into the back of a police van.

Once the giggles had subsided a little (after a 'stern' word from sister), we made our way out of the ward, sister marching ahead, and the ridiculous gang following – Richard making rude jokes, the porter chatting and laughing, the security guard trying to look tough but muffling giggles, and me, casting the occasional stern glance at Richard when he took the blanket off his head and held the sunglasses in the air with a sort of 'ta daa!' motion. He was having a ball, larking about and being naughty. Richard being Richard.

We soon reached the door of the memorial garden. It was a sort of roof garden and very concealed. The security guard insisted on hanging around by the door 'just in case', and the sister took the porter over to the other side of the garden, leaving us alone.

It was a warm, sunny day. There were only a couple of others out on the roof. Richard's chair was parked opposite me, across one of the tables. He closed his eyes, turned his face to the sun, and smiled.

'Ahh. This is nice.'

'Good to be out?' I asked softly.

'Mmm. Sort of.'

He held my hands in his and looked me straight in the eye.

'I'm sorry, Mind.'

'Don't be silly.'

I smiled. But he wasn't ready to stop talking.

'No, I'm really sorry. I love you.'

He leant across the table and kissed me.

'I love you too.'

We looked out at the view across the rooftops towards the centre of Leeds, in silence for a moment.

'So,' he interrupted, 'shall we have a sneaky fag?'

I rolled my eyes. 'I don't believe you!'

'What? A boy's gotta try.'

He persisted for a few minutes with the usual argument, until I pointed out something on the horizon to distract him. Then his mood quite suddenly changed.

'I don't want to be here any more. Can we go back now?'

'Yes, of course, darling.'

The sister had been watching us from afar the whole time, and no sooner did I seek her out with my eyes than she was approaching, the porter by her side.

'Had enough?' she asked with a smile.

Richard was silent.

'Yeah, I think so,' I said, smiling back.

He made a few quips, but was far quieter on our return journey. I wondered whether this small interaction with the outside world had set him back a little. Perhaps he'd realised he really was unwell, and was in shock. He was certainly lost in thought when we got back to the room.

As the days progressed, I had many discussions with the neuro-surgeon Stuart Ross. He was delighted with Richard's recovery, and aware that we were a very long way from home. He felt it would be better to move Richard to a special BUPA hospital in Bristol as soon as possible. We agreed to keep the plans from Richard until we had everything confirmed.

That time in Leeds was difficult for all of us, but especially for Richard's parents. Richard's confusion was dreadful the majority of the time and, although she hid it well, his mum was deeply upset to see her beloved son in such a terrible state. The lad she knew so well was very different, and no one could provide a definitive prognosis. The doctors had decreed that visitors should be kept to a minimum, too. I was there constantly as I was living with Richard in his room. The only other visitors were his parents. His dear dad was always nearby, and took over whenever I left the room. It was a sort of tag team. More than one of us in the room became overwhelming, but individually Richard could cope.

The day before Richard was scheduled to leave Leeds, his parents set off on their long trek back. It was a very emotional and difficult goodbye. Richard's mum put on her bravest face, but had to leave quickly. His dad was steadfast to the last with encouraging words and a positive air. They must have felt so helpless. We all did. There was little we could do except follow the doctor's instructions and hope for the best.

That penultimate day in Leeds was a bit odd. I started to assemble our worldly goods ready for departure; meanwhile, Andy Wilman organised a fully equipped 'hospital plane' to take us from Leeds to Bristol, as the neurosurgeons were concerned it was too far to expect Richard to travel by road. The Yorkshire air ambulance would fly us from the hospital to the local airport, and we'd be met by ambulance on arrival in Bristol. Andy was up and down the corridor all day sorting out travel arrangements. Sourcing the right type of plane hadn't been easy, but then Andy's probably the best man on the planet when it comes to delivering the impossible. Just watch a few of the *Top Gear* challenges and you'll see what I mean. Harrier jump jets, army vehicles, aircraft carriers – nothing is beyond him.

When I explained to Richard the plans for the move to a rehab unit in Bristol he was very excited. But his elation soon clouded.

'So we're going home tomorrow?'

'No, darling, we're going to Bristol. To the rehab unit.'

'Oh yeah. Right. What? For a couple of days?'

'Well, we're not sure. Just see how it goes, OK?'

'Can't we just go home?'

'No, darling, not yet. Hey! Guess how you're getting there.'

'Dunno.'

'A helicopter is collecting you on the roof, then you're transferring to a little plane to fly you to Bristol.'

'You're coming too?' There was a slight air of panic in his voice.

'Obviously.'

'You won't leave me, will you, Mind?'

I knew straight away he wasn't referring to the journey. Richard had moments of great clarity when I believe he realised how unravelled he'd become. For a man who simply doesn't feel fear, he was genuinely scared.

I smiled at him. Hugged him for a long while, feeling him relax into my shoulder, his head bent into the crook of my neck.

'Never,' I whispered.

He squeezed me tight.

I'd never seen him like this, and knew he'd be embarrassed if he had to face me, so I held him for a few moments more. I felt physical pain as I held him. Fighting my own emotions. I couldn't collapse now.

'Cup of tea?' I asked softly.

'Yeah, that'd be good.'

I was careful not to look in his eyes as I made towards the door. When I reached it, I turned to him.

'You OK?'

He smiled. 'Yeah.'

As I closed the door behind me I drew a huge breath and exhaled slowly. One of the nurses was walking towards me along the corridor, and she gave me one of those enquiring looks which, in a glimpse,

asks, Are you OK? Do you need my help? I painted on a smile, and
as she passed I said to her in a high-pitched voice, 'Tea!' She smiled
and winked, and walked on.

I was returning when the sister stopped me briefly for a chat. She
explained that a nurse must accompany Richard on the flight, and
she was thrilled to be coming with us. We joked that she'd have to
hitch-hike back so she'd better not bring too much stuff.

She followed me back to the room to check on Richard. He was
sitting on the bed, smiling and joking with us, when another member
of the team appeared with his medication.

'You won't believe what's been going on outside,' she reported.

A patient had arrived by air ambulance on the roof of the hospital,
and the press had assumed it was Richard's lift, coming to transfer
him. They'd caught wind of rumours about his imminent departure.

'The press are everywhere!' she told us. 'They're on the roofs, in
other buildings – they all went rushing out of the reception area.'

We were really shocked.

'It's as well they were flushed out today,' she continued. 'Security
have done a real sweep. It'll make things easier tomorrow.'

'Oh God, I'm so sorry.' Richard shook his head. 'We've caused
you so much extra work. I'm not only a crap patient but you have
to deal with all this other stuff as well.'

They replied, 'It's nice to have a bit of excitement.'

We all smiled, but after they left Richard continued to worry about
it. We had a long chat about the air ambulance, the money that had
been raised in his name, and of course his popularity (which he
didn't believe at all).

'They can't be that interested in me, for God's sake. I'm just the
little bloke off a car show.'

'Ahem!' I pointed to the sacks and boxes strewn around his room,
brimful with cards, letters and gifts. 'You're the lovely little bloke off

a car show. Don't underestimate how much people care about you.

'But I'm just me.'

'Well, maybe that's why you're special.'

During Richard's time in Leeds a brass-band competition took place. One of the bands taking part approached the hospital to enquire whether they could play a special piece they'd composed for Richard, under his window. The nurses asked if it would be OK, and we said that as long as the other patients didn't mind we thought it was a lovely idea. So it was arranged that the band would start playing after nap time, when all the lights came back on in the ward.

I'd told Richard, and we sat expectantly in his room, awaiting the marvellous sounds of brass. But nothing happened. We decided they were probably coming later, so Richard took a nap and I dashed about making the usual phone calls and tidying up a bit.

At teatime, when the shift changed, one of the nurses came into the room.

'Did you hear the band, then?'

'Erm, no. I suppose they couldn't make it.'

'That's funny,' replied the nurse. 'I'm sure they came.'

She made some enquiries. The band had been to the hospital and played their song for Richard, but unfortunately they'd been directed to the wrong side of the hospital.

It was a shame Richard didn't hear them. It was a very thoughtful gesture. But he laughed and joked about the mix-up for hours, so even though he didn't manage to hear the music, they cheered him up immensely. Thank you.

Chapter 12

THE MOVE TO BRISTOL

I don't remember what time we were leaving, but I recall waking early and foraging through the clothes Alex had kindly bought for Richard, which he was to try on for the first time. A pair of jeans, white T-shirt, pants and socks. It was strange that morning, seeing Richard in real clothes for the first time since the accident.

The nurses came in regularly, checking he was OK and keeping him calm.

I put essentials into bags and made small talk. But Richard was impatient. He just wanted to go.

'What time are they coming?' he asked every ten minutes.

'Don't worry, they'll let us know when the helicopter arrives.'

The plan was to get up to the roof as soon as possible after it landed, but there was no point in us leaving the room until the last minute. If the air ambulance received a call, we'd be kept waiting until they were free.

Andy and Alex were hovering in the corridor. Andy gave me a rundown on the plan of action. Alex had kindly volunteered to clear the contents of the hospital room and transport it all to Bristol by car after we'd left. It was a monumental task. I thanked him for all of his help. As I talked with them I felt quite choked. It was like saying goodbye to the last remnants of the support team. I'd miss them.

Stuart Ross came in to say goodbye. He was astounded at Richard's rate of recovery, but he was anxious to reiterate his advice: 'No work. Your continued recovery depends upon it.'

Both Mr Ross and I knew that Richard's standard promises to rest would be forgotten within minutes. I'd had endless battles trying to prevent him from calling Andy, his colleagues at the *Daily Mirror* and, hardest of all, James and Jeremy. As I explained to Mr Ross, although I completely understood the need to avoid work, Richard's best mates were also his colleagues. What we were asking him to do was effectively cut himself off from his life. Fortunately, Mr Ross agreed a compromise: if I could ensure his conversations didn't turn to the subject of work, he could speak to his mates occasionally. Andy, desperate to do everything in his power to help, was only too happy to follow the plan, as were James and Jeremy.

I'd asked everyone involved in Richard's professional life at the BBC and elsewhere to write to him, explaining that nothing would happen until his return. I could then put the letters in front of him whenever he became worried about work. He needed physical evidence rather than hearsay.

The evening before we were due to leave, Richard had been fretting about work, as he often did. He was sitting on the edge of the bed, a towel around his waist, having just returned from the shower.

'Can you get my phone? I need to call Wilman.'

I have to admit, I was exhausted. This exchange had been repeated on and off all day. I'd taken three showers already, knowing Richard would leave the subject and move on while I was in the bathroom.

'And I need to call the *Mirror*.'

'I've spoken to them, everything's OK.'

I don't know whether it was the tone of my voice, but suddenly, for the first time, Richard's whole persona changed. His face turned to anger.

'Look, I know you think you know what you're doing, but this is my career! My life! Stop speaking to me like I'm an idiot!'

I was so surprised, so overjoyed, I started to cry. Perspective had suddenly arrived. He'd remembered a previous conversation. He'd remembered!

'Richard, I'm so sorry. Of course it's your career.'

But he still looked angry.

'Stop talking to me like that,' he snapped.

Suddenly he was so different. It was fantastic, but at the same time quite shocking.

Speaking as softly as I could, taking care not to sound patronising, I said, 'I don't mean to talk down to you. But, darling, this is the first time you've remembered a conversation. You do remember us talking about this before?'

He looked at me like I was mad.

'Yeah, of course I do. Look. Just, just . . .' He paused, the memory gone again, but his anger still present. 'Just get on with what you're supposed to be doing.'

'OK.'

I rushed into the bathroom and took another shower. I was trembling. Exhilarated and nervous all at once. If his memory had returned, perhaps his anger would remain. Would I walk out to another stony evening? We'd had a few difficult nights when he'd refuse to leave a particular subject and got what the doctors referred to as 'stuck on point'. Moving the conversation on had become increasingly difficult, and he'd been very miserable at times.

Tentatively, I pushed open the adjoining door. He was in bed, gazing vacantly at the TV, which thankfully I'd left on. As I walked through the door he shot me a loving smile.

'You were a long time. Have you shrunk?'

I beamed back at him and inside felt a huge sense of relief. His memory was working its way back, and although still muddled he'd taken another huge step.

We were to go by helicopter to Leeds–Bradford airport. There, a small private plane equipped with stretcher, oxygen and all the medical equipment would fly Richard, the ward sister and me on to a small airport outside Bristol. An ambulance would be waiting to drive the final few miles to The Glen in Clifton which was the only private intensive-care hospital in the area. It boasted a physiotherapy team and gym, and most importantly was close to the brain rehabilitation centre in Frenchay. The team there would take over Richard's care during the difficult weeks ahead.

I was nervous. Even though everyone assured me this was the best course of action – doctors, neurosurgeons, nurses, etc. – I was still worried. Richard had improved so much in the now familiar surroundings of Leeds I was frightened this upheaval might set him back.

When the time came to leave it was a bit of a scramble. Someone appeared and said, 'Time to go.' Richard was being difficult as usual, insisting he could walk.

'Oh no you don't,' said the sister in her firmest tone.

A wheelchair was ready for him and, embarrassed or not, that was to be his mode of transport.

He was pushed by the porter, a security guard and matron in attendance. I'd grabbed a couple of bags and was alongside. Andy came too. Richard kept trying to discuss work with him, but he was constantly putting Richard off the subject.

Such a positive moment, to be moving to a rehabilitation unit, and yet . . . somehow I felt we were leaving everyone behind. There wasn't time to thank them all; I didn't have the words to tell them how much they all meant anyway. We just had to go.

Of course, it wasn't that simple. The sister and I had a battle to stop Richard walking to the helicopter. We both knew he wouldn't make it. Then he wanted to stay in the wheelchair. But I knew Richard, he'd want to mess about or do something daft. If he was in a wheelchair, he'd have to stand up and climb in the helicopter. No way would he manage that. His confidence was high, which was fantastic, but I'd been warned that for him to have a setback while he was progressing so well could be catastrophic.

I didn't wait for the sister. 'Darling, you have to go on the stretcher.'

'No I don't. Come on.'

The sister cottoned on straight away. 'It's the only way they can carry you on the helicopter.'

'Oh, all right then.'

So, thankfully, he was stretchered to the helipad and lifted on to the air ambulance. It was then we discovered it was crewed by the same team who'd rescued him. Richard thanked them for saving his life the previous week, and once aboard set about joking and laughing with the crew, who were clearly delighted to see him so much better. I joined in, but was secretly petrified. He was putting on a show, and I'd back him up, but I was waiting to see what would happen as the trip progressed.

I should mention that I'd only ever been in a helicopter once before. In bad weather. I was petrified, and it had put me off for life. I sat alongside Richard and held his hand. The inside of the helicopter was quite spacious, and Richard wasn't fazed. As we took off, I was nervous he might react. But there was nothing; he simply admired the view.

We noticed that down below us a crowd of photographers had flocked to the front lawn of the hospital and were aiming their cameras skywards, but it was too late. The only photographer to get a shot of Richard leaving had been hiding on a roof opposite the hospital. No one knows how long he'd been there. We wondered later where on earth he'd hidden.

When we landed at Leeds–Bradford airport a small plane awaited us. Richard was soon settled on the stretcher aboard the plane. An oxygen monitor was clipped to his index finger. The sister and I sat opposite each other.

As the plane took off, I watched Richard's face. He was clearly exhausted and looked distant. Even before the oxygen monitor registered any problems, I had already sensed he wasn't right. I hated every moment of that flight. He received oxygen several times during the forty minutes we were in the air. I checked my watch minute by minute.

Several times during the flight I had to wrestle with my own sense of panic. If he was ill on the plane, how would we cope? What could be done? We were stuck up there. I was so grateful when we touched down. Richard insisted on walking to the waiting ambulance, and although it was a slow and difficult few steps, I was proud of his determination.

I've no idea what time we arrived at the BUPA hospital. I remember that Richard fell asleep on contact with his bed. Bristol may have been another step towards recovery, but Stuart Ross had warned me that the worst was yet to come. From a ludicrously quick recovery to date, it would all start to slow down. This was where the hard work began, the frustration started, and the anger could really take hold.

But we'd arrived. Richard was safe. It was time to start the next phase.

Chapter 13

DID YOU KNOW
SWANS MATE FOR LIFE?

There is a scene in Stephen King's *Misery* where the main character wakes to find that his ankles, which his less-than-friendly hostess has recently broken for him with a mallet, are hurting badly. As I drifted between coma and consciousness in intensive care in Leeds General Infirmary, that scene haunted me. I could see a nurse holding a plastic cup. I was in bed. I couldn't understand who she was, why she was there, or why I was in bed. She offered me the cup. It was a dose of morphine. Did I want it?

In the Stephen King book, the character is offered morphine to dull the pain of his shattered ankles. The bloke with the ankles compares his pain to the jagged, blackened piles of wood sticking out of the sea bed on the coast. The morphine, he explains, is the sea, and it washes over the pain, masking and hiding it. I thought what a beautiful metaphor this was as the nurse leaned closer with the drugs, and I felt happy in the freshly laundered scent of the hospital sheets. The morphine must have swept over whatever pain was troubling me in my coma and I drifted back out of consciousness again. I don't remember the pain. There was only relief. And sleep.

The ground looked rough but friendly. The path twisted ahead, tempting me on. On either side, the mountains rose and the valleys between lay cool and dark. I walked on and felt naughty. I was being bad by following this lovely path. Like I was back at school, doing something the teachers didn't want me to. It felt like the Lake District, my favourite place in the world. I sensed, but never saw, tiny flowers on long velvet stems bobbing in the grass nearby. There was no noise, just the occasional gust of a breeze that set the grass waving. I was happy to be there and didn't want to give in to all the people who were a bit cross about my journey. But the pressure of their disapproval mounted. I could sense that their mood was changing to anger. I knew that I was in trouble. Mindy was cross, and I didn't want her to be. So I stopped messing about and did as I was told. I came back.

Mindy was, indeed, cross. I didn't know it, but she had been standing over me in the intensive-care unit, bellowing my name. I have learned since that things had been looking very bad for a while and Mindy had asked the nurse if she could shout at me to see if I responded. I don't think the nurse knew what she was letting herself in for. She told Mindy that it might help. That was all Mindy needed to hear, and she launched into a barrage of shouting and yelling, urging me to respond and come back. I did. The medical observations made a turn for the better, and I was safe, though still unconscious. The nurses and doctors satisfied themselves that my condition had stabilised once more and were happy for me to drift through my coma. With no more shouting.

I remember nothing clearly of being in Leeds General Infirmary. I owe my life to the people there but I can remember nothing of being under their care. Time spent in a coma is time spent in an entirely different sort of consciousness. On many occasions, I am told, I woke, but I cannot distinguish those times from the distant memories of dreams and fantasy. Two worlds become blurred: the world in your head and the world that recently hurt you so badly. It was a long time spent living between two worlds.

Bed was nice. I liked being there. But I had been in a crash, a bad one. It was easier, finally, to accept and believe it. Even though there was no evidence to support it. Apart from being in what, clearly, was a hospital, there was nothing else to back up Mindy's claims. I could move; there was no pain; everything worked. But I felt sad. Something was wrong. I needed to sleep. So I did.

Distantly, in flashes, I remembered. The jet car had crashed. I had been fighting to save it. Something had gone wrong with the steering. I could feel the panic rising as I fought and recalled the sense that I was on the point of losing my fight. And then something else had gone wrong. I thought I was going to die. I hadn't been scared, just sad. There had been nothing more I could do but die. Now I was in hospital. I hadn't died. But I had hurt my brain; damaged the very place where I lived.

It's the most intimate way to be hurt; the most personal attack imaginable. I was reduced to thoughts, to patterns and pictures, but nothing solid. I had been forced back into the very cave I came from and I hid at the back, lashing out at anything that came near. My body had been hurt, but that didn't matter to me now. I wasn't a body, I was something else. I had to fight back. I needed to sleep. It was a dark battle, and a bitter one. I needed strength. I needed to sleep. So I did.

Mindy was talking to me again. Slowly. The jet car had crashed and I had banged my head really badly. I held her – or she held me – and I felt sad. But I believed her now. I was in hospital and I was there because of what I had done to my head. I was important; I was the patient. The world revolved around me. Meals came and went. I slept when I wanted to. A nurse came round every now and then and stuck needles in me, but it was a small price to pay for being the centre of everyone's world.

A jet engine started up right by my head. There were many people around me, busy doing important stuff. Mindy was with me. I focused on her. It was exciting, whatever we were doing. We were with a group of people. I was in a gang again. This was good. The jet engine screamed more urgently. 'Last thing I remember hearing was a jet engine,' I said. Someone laughed. I was showing off. That felt great. I had been in a crash with a jet engine. That was why I was up here on the roof getting into a helicopter. And then nothing.

For two weeks, little flashes of consciousness meshed together, out of time and sequence, to make up a sort of thread that I lived along. I did not believe what had happened. We weren't kids any more, we were grown-ups. So how could it go wrong? Finally, almost two weeks after getting into the jet car for the last time, I accepted that it had crashed. Mindy had explained it to me again and again and I had not believed her, even though I had no other theory to explain why I was in bed. But finally, in the hospital room in Bristol, holding Mindy's hand, I accepted it. I felt guilty about the crash. Maybe I had done something wrong? Was it my fault? Did I go too fast? But at least now I believed what Mindy said. And that made things a lot easier to connect together.

It was easy to accept in the end. If the last thing you recall is the sound of a jet engine starting up just inches behind your head before being fired up a runway at 300 mph in a dragster – well, your mind is hardly surprised if you come out of a coma in hospital a week or two later. How much harder must it be for patients who come out of a coma to find they no longer recognise the woman everyone tells them is their wife and the last thing they remember is riding a bicycle to the shop for bread? When I was well enough to be able to process the thought and consider it, this would be the first of many, many lessons in the business of recovery from brain-damage. It's not just what you've done; it's important how you've done it. My mind had to cope with the aftermath of the accident, but at least it was spared the difficulty of trying to understand how a seemingly mundane act could change the way you look at the world. I was lucky: I had hurt myself in such an exceptional and unusual set of circumstances that it was easier to accept.

Mindy was a constant presence, and without realising it I came to rely on her as I relied on air and water. She was more than sustenance, she was my refuge, shield and strength; she was my interpreter, the conduit for my difficult and confusing emotions. How these roles drained her, I can only ever try to imagine. When she left the room, I stopped coping. She was living for two of us.

I stirred in my bed. This was going to be OK. I would be a model patient – calm, relaxed, cooperative and, of course, patient. Maybe that's where the name comes from. I wanted to be the best patient they had ever had, one they would talk about for years to come. I wanted to show off again.

I had been a patient only once before, when as a six-year-old I had stayed in hospital for a few days for minor surgery on my eardrums. The isolation, the loneliness and the home-sickness returned to me in waves. Some aspect of the hospital's plumbing had been particularly ancient, and the pipes had moaned and mooed all night, like a herd of cattle wandering the wards. Their cries had kept me pinned to the starched sheets with fear. They returned now to haunt my long nights in a hospital hundreds of miles and three decades away from the last one I stayed in. I would sleep deeply until, for some reason, I woke and lay silently, feeling once more the night-time dread of a scared six-year-old boy.

I devoted every waking hour to trying to persuade the doctors that I was ready to go home. I wanted to return to normality. To get back to a life in which I went off to work, did daft stuff and came home again to Mindy and the kids with stories and tales. My memory was still badly damaged. This was not damage to my deeper memories – I knew who I was, I recognised my children, and I recognised my parents and brothers; it was my day-to-day memory, which extended only to a few minutes. A conversation would be forgotten within moments, and I might ask the same question dozens of times. This only added to the state of confusion that nagged at me, and, I suspect, made me difficult to be around.

———

Richard was very tired after his arrival at Bristol. The journey had taken its toll. He was very argumentative, and as I was also tired, it wasn't the easiest transition.

Rick Nelson, the neurosurgeon taking over his care, came to visit. He had a wonderful manner. He was calm and softly spoken, and he listened patiently to Richard's animated exchanges, all the while glancing across at me. He was gauging the validity of the person in front of him, and guessed correctly that this wasn't the true Richard. He also sensed that I couldn't be honest in Richard's presence. At the end of the discussion, Rick asked Richard's permission to have a chat alone with me to discuss his progress as I saw it. He agreed. I felt I'd been given permission to disclose vital information.

I was Richard's ally. I'd stood alongside him as sword and shield; if I suddenly appeared to switch allegiance, all trust would dissipate. Rick had provided the ultimate solution. Discussing my husband's condition behind his back felt terrible, but I knew it was vital the medical team were aware of all the facts.

Rick immediately recognised textbook characteristics in Richard. He was desperately trying to demonstrate how articulate, how well recovered he was, and yet ... ask him what town he was in, and there was instant confusion. Richard was a very intelligent man, but his mind remained jumbled. The doctors compared the state of his mental function to a filing cabinet that had been knocked to the floor: all the files were scattered about, the papers spread all over the room. We were trying to help him put it all back together. It was a slow and difficult task. He would get frustrated; he'd become angry and despairing; but patience was the key. And rest. His brain was exhausted, and the best therapy was sleep. The most dangerous factor was work. If he overtaxed his brain too soon, he would suffer a relapse. That would set him back dreadfully, and Rick spared no punches. It would be hard to claw back from there.

―――――

Post-traumatic amnesia helped alleviate the boredom. This, in turn, made life a little easier for people looking after me. I could happily read the same newspaper a dozen times, forgetting each time I picked it up that I had read it only minutes earlier. It also meant that I was easy to cater for. I would read the lunch menu, spot that cottage pie was available and exclaim that it was my favourite and ask for it. When it arrived, ten minutes or so later, I would forget that I had ordered it from the menu and be delighted that it was my favourite dish and ask how the staff could possibly have known it. When the dinner menu appeared, I would find that it had cottage pie on it, and we would repeat the process. After several days of this, I learned later that Mindy asked the staff to tell me that, sadly, the cottage pie was all gone. When they told me this for the second, fifth and tenth times, I had, of course, forgotten and was disappointed but not broken-hearted.

By the time I understood post-traumatic amnesia, that it might mean that a patient such as me could be left temporarily with a memory that stretched back only a few minutes, I was getting over it. But the confusion that remained, the fact that I could not trust my own perception of the world and my own thoughts, was a frightening state to be in. To know that I was in such a state made things worse. With every stage of increasing awareness, I grew more scared. At this point in the long process of recovery, I knew enough to know that I had hurt my brain. But I didn't know how it might be affecting me. I could have been dreaming the entire thing. At least now I accepted that I had suffered an injury and that I was in a hospital so that I might get better.

But I still wanted to go home. Badly.

———

There was little to compare between my role at Leeds and that at Bristol. Although I slept with Richard every night and was with him as much as possible, we were close to home, closer to the girls, and clearly I should be with them, too. A routine was devised which allowed for a late-afternoon nap for Richard. That was my time to rush home, see the girls, and return before he became too distressed.

It wasn't terribly successful. Often the hospital would call my mobile before I'd even reached home. I'd run into the house, try to enjoy a fun time with the girls, but all the while preoccupied with a nagging sense of urgency to get back to him. We'd chat about their day as they splashed in the bath, but the bedtime story was shorter, and the 'goodnights' far more difficult. They'd phone Daddy to wish him 'goodnight' and then I was off again. The second I left their rooms, I ran down the stairs and continued running to the car. The keys were never removed from the ignition.

Journey time was taken up with phone calls. I had two phones, which was useful. At least one was always charging. I listened to messages and returned as many as possible. Conversations were timed to fit the maximum in. So many dear friends were desperate to know how Richard really was, but naturally my first call was always to his parents. I'd update them on progress, and they'd filter the news to other members of the family. My mum was next. Her comforting words gave me strength.

Occasionally I'd feel tired, but determination drove me on, and the desperate longing to be back with Richard. It was like leaving a child in a strange place with kind but unfamiliar company. I sensed he was forever fighting panic. Controlling himself. Being brave.

———

There is an expression the doctors wear when they come into your room in a unit like the one at Bristol, half-wary and half-defensive. As soon as they crossed the threshold I would spring to attention and begin a torrent of talk as I tried to prove my return to health and sanity and regain my freedom.

'Morning, Richard, how are you?'

'Well, thank you. Much better. Bit worried about this weather though – looks like a spot of low pressure heading our way.'

I made a sweeping gesture to my right, meaning to encompass the window. Which was to my left.

'Did you know swans mate for life?'

'No, Richard. Do you know what day it is?'

'No.'

And I didn't. I could recall stuff from years ago; random facts and memories popped up with incredible clarity. Sometimes I could close my eyes and suddenly be in a place I last visited decades ago. But I could get no grip on the present. My sense of time and place was badly distorted. Facts, ideas, meanings slipped from my grasp and evaded my best attempts to pin them down. Eventually, I got used to the business of not being able to answer simple questions, but at first it was terrifying.

I became aware that there was something wrong with me that stopped me understanding. And I was scared. Brain-damage affected the way I thought about things. It might be affecting the way I thought about brain-damage. And I didn't know what day it was. Or where I was. The panic that rose whenever I failed to answer a question that I knew I should understand got in the way of my thoughts and made things worse. I would be screaming inside my head because I knew that this should be easy.

I shall never forget those days of struggling in what was a clinically confused state. I shall always try to hold on to the memory of how hard it was to make sense of the world. It made me horribly self-centred; childish, like a toddler who cannot comprehend that there can be a will in the world other than their own. I shall try to keep these memories close, because it will for ever change the way I deal with people who are likewise confused. Sometimes it was rather pleasant to bounce along, wondering what was for lunch when I had only ordered it five minutes earlier, and wondering if Mindy would come back and we could see everyone else at the party I thought we were at. The distress was, sadly, to be felt by the people closest to me. It is far harder, I am sure, to visit someone you know and love and see them in such a confused state for weeks on end than it is to be the one happily asking where the bar is in a hospital ward. But among those flashes of insight and awareness there were some deeply frightening moments. My heart goes out to anyone now similarly afflicted, and for whom the prognosis might not be so bright as mine proved to be.

As my memory became better and my mind relaxed into something closer to a normal state, there were some big emotions waiting to get hold of me. Early in my stay at Bristol, I was hit by a huge avalanche of guilt. I suddenly felt horribly aware of the worry and pain I had caused Mindy, my daughters, my brothers and, of course, my parents. The sense that I had done something very stupid and upset a lot of people by doing it hovered in the background of my jumbled thoughts.

I woke up, lying in a bed once more. But this time I knew that I was in hospital, that I was hurt. And I wanted to see my parents. I wanted to explain to them that it wasn't my fault, that I hadn't messed up, that something had gone wrong with the car and that I had not done anything wrong. I wanted to say that I was sorry and they mustn't worry. It was just like every time I had fallen off a bicycle or a garage roof as a child. I never worried that they would shout at me when I hurt myself as a child; they never would. But I knew, deep down, in the way that children do, that it would upset them. I remembered walking into the kitchen with my hand torn to pieces when I fell off my brother's bicycle. I remembered seeing the white bones and cartilage in my fingers and the red, ripped flesh. But more clearly even than the pain, I remembered seeing my mother's face and her struggle to remain calm and help me when probably all she wanted to do was scream in horror that her baby was hurt.

Well, how would she feel now? This was worse than that. And I also now had a much better understanding of what a parent feels when they see their child hurt. I had children of my own, and once the switch of parenthood is thrown, it changes you for ever. I was lying in that hospital bed as both a ten-year-old child holding up an injured hand to his mother, and as a father myself, who now had a much better idea about the pain a parent can feel. I never managed to voice these feelings to my parents; somehow it just came out wrong when I tried. But I felt such a weight of guilt I thought it would crush me where I lay.

This guilt is a common thing among people recovering from head injuries such as mine, and from many bodily injuries too. Much later, still crawling back towards health, I would be hit by a second avalanche of guilt, this time centred on how I had been so lucky when many people are not. I would lie awake, pinned down by the knowledge that I had been through a massive accident and emerged alive when people are far more badly hurt falling down the stairs. That guilt is, perhaps, harder to fight against, and I still carry it today. But as I lay in bed in Bristol, the only guilt I felt was for the worry I had caused my parents, brothers and wife. They all worked unbelievably hard to protect me from it, and I thank them for that.

With my returning memory, the problem of filling my days became more pressing. But I wasn't lying in bed dreaming of getting back to work. I didn't want to go back; I couldn't really understand the concept of work anyway, not in an adult way. I knew that work was something I did out there in the real world and that I had to be grown-up and that I had children and a wife and that my work paid for a house for us all to live in. But I couldn't imagine actually doing it. I wanted to fill my time with things I enjoyed. I wanted to play. I had regressed until I felt and thought like a child, and was happy to do so.

It was raining outside, and I watched the drops track their wiggly paths down the window of my hospital room. I looked at the cars lined up below, studied the colours and shapes of them, and wanted to walk among them. I wanted to touch their metal curves, feel the raindrops on their thick-painted panels. I wanted to step out into the world and experience it for myself. Above all else, I wanted to go to a shopping centre and buy something. I wanted to walk among familiar shop frontages, see their colourful signs, and I wanted to hear the voices of other people. I wanted to see the hustle and bustle and be part of it all.

In my mind, I drifted back to childhood trips to the Bull Ring shopping centre in Birmingham. We were buying school shoes for a new term. We turned a corner and walked down some steps. There was a stand selling bags. I didn't want one, but I admired their shiny surfaces and glistening buckles while my mum chatted to the man selling them. Suddenly I was in front of another stall, selling food. I wasn't interested, and I thought about Batman. I thought that when I got home I would make a model of Batman's car out of Lego. I would gather together as many black bricks as I could find; those big blocks that held wheels on would be useful. I wished I could think of a way of making the blade that the real Batmobile had in the front to cut through any wires that got in the way during a chase. I could use the green wire Dad used sometimes to hold plants up. But no, it wouldn't look right. It never did when you mixed real things in with Lego. It just looked silly. But the fins, the fins I would give this Batmobile would be fantastic. They would be huge and sleek and pointed.

Mum was calling me and my brother Andy. We had to go. We ran up a concrete ramp past the shop windows.

In a flash, the scene changed. I was in Solihull now, closer to home. We ran down the ramp instead, into the big hall underneath. This was Mel Square, the centre of town, where the big fountains leapt from the square pool and splashed back into the shallow water. The ramp was cobbled with stones or ridges and we had to take lots of tiny steps. We ran and shouted, laughing as our voices wobbled. Mum thought it was funny too. On the ramp, we all laughed and our voices echoed off the stony sides and filled the hall below.

I looked away from the window of my hospital room and I wanted to go outside. I wanted to walk into a shop and treat myself to something special. I wanted to buy a new Lego set and savour the moment when the tiny bricks tumbled out of the crinkly plastic bag in a multi-coloured cascade, ready to form into the picture on the front of the box with the help of the shiny, crisp instructions that had yet to be unfolded. That was it. I wanted Lego. It had taken me through my childhood. I had spent nearly every waking hour trying to build the cars and bikes I dreamed of riding and driving for real. My creations with their bobbly tops and mismatched colours would set off on huge adventures through jungles under the coffee table or into the dark and threatening canyon between Dad's chair and the wall. I craved that escape now. I knew I wasn't a ten-year-old boy any more, that I was a thirty-six-year-old man in a hospital. But I knew also that I was ill and allowed to do things if they made me feel better. I wanted to play.

Seldom do we have, as adults, the time to spend gazing out of windows wondering about ourselves and our own lives. I had returned to a stage when, perhaps as a young teenager, I could while away hours thinking about life and my place in it. My world slowly narrowed in focus until it encompassed just the room I was in. Like a child, I could fill hours peering into corners, looking at things in a way I had not done for decades. There was never usually time to just sit and stare. Maybe the process of recovery itself necessitated this, as well as the re-treading of old ground to remember who I was.

There was a light knock, the door swung open, and Dr John Holloway walked in. A tall, gentle-looking man, I was happy to see his friendly face and to chat with him. We spoke about how I felt. I said I was fine. While we spoke, I noticed him glancing down to the side of the bed. I saw what was capturing his attentive glance – a book of prayer that had been sent in by a well-wisher.

'Are you reading this?' he asked.

'Well, I glance at it.' I wanted to show that I had big spiritual thoughts. I wanted, as always, to show off. 'I read through it sometimes.'

'Right.'

He was sounding me out. Looking for something. I stayed silent. John waited quietly and thumbed the pages.

'Good. We keep an eye out for sudden, you know, surges of enthusiasm for things at this point.'

'Oh, I see. No, I haven't suddenly found religion, if that's what you mean.'

We knew each other well enough now to talk about how accidents such as mine might affect people. I enjoyed these talks, and I suspect John used them to gauge my recovery. He explained that sudden obsessions can leap up from nowhere. They might be to give away all your money, give up a stressful job, or to become fervently religious. It is, perhaps not surprisingly, common for people who have been near to death to return from that place with a new-found religious conviction. This is doubtless a fine thing, but to a mind in as delicate a state as mine, it might also become complicated. I assured John that I still clung to the same ill-formed and nebulous beliefs on the subject of God and the afterlife as I'd always had. It was a subject I would relish talking about further, but this, perhaps, was not the time. John seemed relieved, and after a few more comforting words he left the room. I slipped into a deep sleep.

Mindy arrived. I came alive. By this stage she had begun to explain that my crash had caused a bit of a stir in the media. It was no longer in the news bulletins, so I never picked up on it during my long hours in front of the TV, but there had, she explained, been quite a splash. I don't remember her showing me the newspaper coverage and the doctors were still anxious that I should be protected from too many stimuli. Leafing through newspaper headlines about my imminent demise and subsequent narrow escape might prove to be a bit too much. This was still, as far as I was concerned, an intensely private matter involving me, my family and the medical staff helping me back to health.

I knew that the *Top Gear* team had been to see me when I was still in Leeds General Infirmary, but I had no memory of the event. We are a close-knit team and I wasn't surprised that they had felt the need to be there and see me for themselves.

We have joked many times that we all work in a playground for grown-ups. We all pretend to be working, but we mess about in cars and with TV cameras just as we mostly all did as kids. And one of us had fallen over in the playground badly. They all wanted to see how their friend was. It would be exactly the same if any of us were hurt. The fact that they had visited meant a lot to me then, but I was unable to access any details in my bruised and battered brain.

So the newspapers were kept away, but Mindy did allow a gradual flow of the thousands of letters, cards and gifts from well-wishers. They arrived at the hospital in sack loads, and each day Mindy would bring in as much of the post as the doctors would allow, until gradually we got to the point where I could happily plough through them alone. And it felt wonderful. I did not open them as a television personality, a celebrity tearing open fan mail and soaking up the adulation of people he had never met; I opened and read each card and letter as just a bloke sitting in a hospital bed being wished well by thousands of kind friends who seemed to mean what they wrote with real sincerity.

Many of the letters were from people who had been similarly injured. Perhaps they had not suffered their injuries under the same circumstances, but they had faced similar battles to get well and were keen to share their experiences with a fellow sufferer. I read an account from a young teenage lad who suffered a head injury after falling off his motorcycle. He was, from his letter, clearly a young tough-nut who embraced life and enjoyed the thrill of riding his dirt bike competitively. Yet he felt compelled to write and share the story of his accident, and to talk about how deeply it had affected him and how hard it was to recover. In doing so with such honesty and candour, he rendered himself vulnerable in a way that must have been uncomfortable to a teenager. He didn't write to the bloke off *Top Gear* to tell him about how fast he went on his bike; he wrote to tell him not to be scared that he had injured his brain, because he had done the same thing and got better. It was a source of comfort beyond words.

His note, and the thousands of other sincere and thoughtful letters and cards written by people from all over the world, were the most touching acts of kindness I could have imagined. Each contributed to the restoration of my shattered confidence. My heart went out then, and it does now, to those who are far more deserving of such help and do not have the benefit of it. For me, the hours could be passed happily, lying on my bed reading these letters slowly and with care, as you do a letter from a friend.

Mindy arrived again. She had probably only been down a corridor to talk with the doctors or to make a phone call, but for me, like a dog, my sense of the passage of time was limited. When she wasn't in the room, she just wasn't there. It didn't make any difference if she was gone for minutes or hours, I just wanted her to come back. This time, she walked through the door carrying a box under her arm. It was large, brightly coloured, and I knew what it was more by instinct than by reading the familiar red-and-white logo. It was a box of Lego. Mindy explained that James May had bought it for me. He and I share a love of engineering and construction that can be enjoyed by considering the inner workings of an F1 engine or just by messing about with old motorbikes. He had guessed, rightly, that my confused mind would relish the prospect of the simple but involved process of building a child's toy.

It was a model of a tractor. A big green one. The bags of bricks and plastic cogs felt as temptingly lovely as I had dreamed.

The instructions were colourful and, for me at that point, complex enough to demand my full attention. I can only imagine what Mindy must have felt as she watched me throw myself into a project aimed at a child thirty years my junior. For me, the world came alive in a brightly coloured, technically demanding challenge. I built the tractor. People came into my room and went. Nurses visited to stick pins in my stomach that would, I was assured, do me good. Doctors visited and people brought food. I concentrated on the task and revelled in the achievement. Dr Holloway went as far as to say that the process of translating two-dimensional instructions into three-dimensional models might even be beneficial. It would, he explained, help me rediscover my sense of spatial awareness and my concentration. This was all I needed to hear. I pleaded with Mindy to bring more Lego. She saw the enthusiasm in my face, and ran to the shops.

———

Richard became increasingly frustrated with his confinement.

'Why can't I go for a walk? I just need to get out. I want to go to a shopping centre and buy daft stuff, just go shopping. Please? Why can't I go shopping?'

Richard hates shopping. Loathes it. Avoids it at all costs. So why on earth would he now have this uncontrollable urge?

He agreed to give me a list. I'd go. The list read:

Classic Bike magazine
Classic Car magazine
Pen and paper for letter writing
Lego set

I dashed out to Cribbs Causeway, a large shopping complex just outside Bristol. The first three items were easy. The Lego, ridiculously, was a nightmare. I was jogging from one end of the enormous mall to the other and into every shop I vaguely imagined might stock it, but to no avail. In desperation, I went into Boots. In the children's department there were just a couple of suitable models, a boat and a remote-control car. I bought the boat and two of the cars.

To compensate for my lack of Lego, I spent ten minutes in a sweet shop, buying all of Richard's favourites in ridiculous quantities. I was constantly glancing at my watch, and I knew time was passing far too quickly. I had an hour to get back to Richard, settle him and leave for home.

Shoppers wandering calmly, browsing the halls, stared at me as I ran at full tilt through the complex, down the stairs and out to my car. I was hot and sweaty, dishevelled with an air of slight madness. I yelled at slow-moving traffic and made swift progress when the road cleared. I managed a fairly relaxed cup of tea with Richard as we looked through his goodies before leaving again on the return trip home to Gloucestershire.

———

Within days, my room had been transformed, filled with brightly coloured boxes of Lego. I buried myself in my new-found work. The place looked like a toyshop. Or, better still, like my childhood fantasy of a Lego-testing facility. And I was chief tester.

Mindy arrived once more, stepping into the chaos and smiling as I looked up from the floor where I was busily building a ship. She had brought the kids. My heart leapt. I asked them if they would like to join me and play. They said yes, and crouched down next to me.

With Izzy and Willow around, I knew my place again. I was their father; I was in hospital because I had suffered a head injury and I had to try not to upset them. I loved them more than anything else in the world, but I couldn't go home with them.

With no sense of the passage of time, I was unaware how long they had been with me when Mindy announced that they must leave. I held the girls tightly; they clung to me and I to them. I walked with them to the door and, on a whim, followed them into the corridor beyond. I was still unsteady on my feet, but was not going to show it. We walked to the lift, the four of us. Mindy pressed the button and, too quickly, the lift arrived. In the pause before the doors shut, I smiled at them as they stood there, framed by the metal doorway. They smiled back.

As the doors began to slide together, Izzy broke her gaze away from mine and turned her head to look up at Mindy. Her smile crumbled and her eyes filled with tears. She had held them back for as long as she could and now she could hold them back no longer. As she looked up to Mindy for support, her resolve not to cry failed and she succumbed. She was a six-year-old girl missing her daddy very much, scared and worried. I looked at Mindy as the doors shut with a soft click, ending the scene, and I stared for some time at the anonymous blank space where my family had been. I wept too as I walked back to my room, my powerlessness only emphasised by the feel of the hospital floor under my bare feet as I trudged the few steps back up the corridor.

The second the lift doors closed, Izzy collapsed on to my legs and burst into uncontrollable sobs. I was on my knees with her in an instant. I praised her bravery and was completely astounded by her. She instinctively knew how to help her beloved daddy. She was giving all her tiny body could muster for him, solely for him. At just six years old, she had been more thoughtful and caring than many adults. She even composed herself so that by the time we reached the back door some two minutes later, she could walk out and raise a hand to the windows above, knowing that Daddy was watching, encouraging her little sister to do the same. Ela and I followed suit, the tears flowing down all our faces, save Willow, who thankfully didn't notice.

'Oh, Izzy, baby, well done,' I told her.

She simply nodded, the tears dripping from her face.

'Are you OK, Izzy?' asked Willow.

Izzy nodded at Willow, and we drove home. Together, but without Daddy. For Izzy it was dreadful, but somewhere, somehow, she understood. This was the way it had to be – for a while. But as I told her again and again, 'He'll get better, Iz – I promise.' She'd nod, and cry, and hug me. But she's from a tough stable and she believed me, and believed in her father. She made Willow her responsibility, and I believe she determined to stay strong for her little sister, who didn't understand. I only know this: a little girl decided of her own volition to become more than a daughter. She became, as Richard described her, 'his mate'.

It was wonderful to be home with them. As we drove through the gate, I could hear the dogs barking wildly from the kitchen – a sound I suddenly realised I'd missed. Home. Ela and the girls opened the front door and we immediately set the dogs free from the kitchen. I was surrounded by bouncing, barking, tail-wagging excitement. TG grabbing my hand in her mouth, Captain leaping up at me, Pablo barking and Crusoe stretching forward and yowling, each of them desperate to impress their welcome upon me. Willow and Izzy laughed and giggled.

'I think they missed you, Mindy!' Ela said with a smile.

The girls and I ran outside with them all and watched them as they galloped off up the hill next to our house. Barking, scampering, happy to be free.

We went over to see Hattie, our enormous outdoor dog. She slobbered and harrumphed and lay on her back for her belly to be scratched.

'Ohhh! Hattie Pudding!'

Willow gently stroked the dog's chest as she lay licking her lips in complete ecstasy.

Hattie is a guard dog, and she'd spent a great deal of the past week barking at the many strangers at the gate. She was hoarse as a result, her usual deep bark a little husky and high-pitched. She was at least three times Willow's size, yet with the children she was as gentle as a lamb. They were her babies, and she took her role as protector very seriously. Apparently, when the children left the house she grew silent, awaiting their return, her front paws resting on the top of the five-bar gate at the entrance to her kennel area, watching for a car.

We all returned to the house and Ela made a quick supper for the girls while I dashed around upstairs, grabbing clothes for Richard. The girls were in the playroom, lost in a game, and I just had time for a quick chat with Ela before Izzy joined us. She saw the suitcase in the hall. Her face fell, and she hugged my legs.

'Oh, Mummy, do you have to go again?'

I picked her up and carried her into the hall where Willow might not find us. I put her down on the stairs and sat next to her. We had one of our 'grown-up chats'. It was something Richard often did with her. We talked about Daddy, how she felt, and why I needed to help him now. Just for a while, just until he was better.

'I miss Daddy,' she sobbed.

'Daddy misses you, baby. He misses everything, but we'll help him get better, won't we?'

She nodded, and wiped her face dry with her sleeve, then ran her nose along her arm.

'Eeeew! Bogey slime!'

I laughed, she giggled, we hugged.

'I love you, Mummy.'

I held on to her. I couldn't prevent my own tears. But she didn't notice. Or at least, she pretended not to.

We joined Ela and Willow at the table for supper, but before it was finished the hospital called. Richard was anxious. My time at home was fast running out.

———

Like many people, I guess, I am never happy in an institution. But here, in Bristol, the order and regularity of the days, the constant presence of caring professionals, and the sense that I was in the right place doing the right thing to get better, helped soothe away some of the fear and confusion. I became, perhaps for the first time, institutionalised. And I grew happier. I woke up naturally in the mornings, chatted with nurses and doctors who cared about me, ate breakfast and played with Lego. At lunchtime, food was brought. I ate it, slept for a few hours, woke and played with Lego again, and wondered what was for tea.

In a sense, the transformation was complete; I was ten years old again, and quite happy to be so.

And at this point I began to miss my two brothers in a way I hadn't for decades. I wanted them to be there with me, sitting cross-legged on the floor, trying to decide what model to build next or wondering what was coming up on the telly. They have jobs they work at to support their families and busy, complicated adult lives. But I missed them as the kids I grew up with. I had now drifted back into childhood, and I wondered where my two best mates were.

I have spoken with them since and learned that, in many ways, they had been afflicted with similar emotions. Whatever happens to any of the three of us in our lives, part of us will always be the same three young tearaways who rode bicycles round 'the Triangle', made dens on 'the field' at the back of the house, and played with toy cars in 'the ditch'. They had visited me many times in hospital over the past few weeks, of course. But I held on to no memories of those early visits. On later occasions they arrived to find me confused and bewildered. I guess I was wondering who these two grown men were and where my brothers had gone.

But these thoughts, though intense, passed quickly. I could happily distract myself. I had, for a day or so, been building a model of the Batmobile. Dr Holloway still popped in regularly, and on one occasion he asked how the Batmobile was going. I began to explain that it was pretty tricky in places and you had to pay close attention to the instructions. I had taken his enquiry to mean that he too was in the process of assembling a Batmobile and was, perhaps, struggling. I felt sure that he would benefit from my many years of modelling experience and I was happy to share it with him. It was only after a good few minutes of giving patient and very comprehensive instruction in the finer points of assembling the Lego model that I realised he was humouring me. And I was embarrassed for the first time in a while. Which was probably a good sign.

At some point, someone identified a need in me for physical exercise. I run nearly every day as a rule and benefit from it physically but also mentally. Maybe I had shown signs of stagnating in my tiny room full of Lego. Given that I had suffered pretty much no bodily injuries apart from those to my brain, I remained in reasonably good shape. But I had lost a lot of weight. A week or two of being fed through a needle in your arm will do that to you.

I was asked if I would like to go to the hospital gym and I bounced up and down like the ten-year-old I felt myself to be. Mindy brought in my running kit, ready for the big day. When the time came, a physiotherapist lady collected me from my room and took me down the stairs to another floor. This was the furthest I could recall travelling for what felt like years, and I hungrily absorbed every new and strange feature. A fire extinguisher, a liquid-soap dispenser and a yellow bin leapt out from corners to ignite my senses.

We walked through to a small room. Inside were a few bits and pieces of gym equipment and some pale-green crash mats laid out on the floor. I was taken through some yoga moves. We stretched and talked. The physiotherapist was very friendly and kind, and I tried to show off by being really good at yoga. I wasn't. And then she asked if I would like to use the rowing machine. I most certainly would, and I pounced on it eagerly. After four minutes of pulling I was pretty much exhausted. It doesn't take long for whatever physical fitness you have to drain away. Mine had disappeared down the plughole the moment I took to a hospital bed. But it felt wonderful to be exerting myself physically again. And the benefit was more mental than physical.

This was the first time I could really pit myself against something and be allowed to struggle. It was as much about the realisation that the doctors felt I was well enough to work up a bit of a sweat as it was about the exercise itself. The rowing machine suffered from a piercing squeak. Over the next few days I would wonder if my frantic rowing and the accompanying squeak was keeping other patients awake. I felt bad but I rowed on, slowly increasing my stamina. Mindy did everything she could to encourage this gentle exercise, listening patiently when I explained breathlessly and proudly that I was up to seven minutes' rowing and was now being allowed to use the running machine too.

I dreamed of being able to take off on my own and run outside in the real world. I dreamed of running along tree-lined paths scattered with big yellow leaves and clambering over fences to sprint across wide, muddy fields under skies with real weather in them. As my trainers slapped down on the treadmill, in my mind I breathed in the natural and vital smells of the real world.

I was going to leave the hospital. But I couldn't go home. By now, it had been explained to me that our house was ringed with reporters and TV crews, and the doctors were worried about how I might react. Dr Holloway explained that every single thing that caught my attention or happened around me must be considered a stimulus. Because of the fragile state of my mind we had to be careful. There was no dipstick to slot into my brain and tell the doctors if I was now liable to convulsions or mental complications. But there were statistics.

Thousands of cases are recorded and examined, as much for the benefit of subsequent patients as the one under examination. It's sad that there are so many cases of brain injury to record, but at least the resulting statistics can help predict problems that, history has shown, might arise as a patient goes through the recovery process and beyond. And these statistics told the doctors that with a brain injury of the severity of mine, there were dangers associated with over-stimulation. Leaving the security and predictability of the hospital would be shocking enough, but to go home and be confronted with a horde of eager reporters, TV cameras and flashguns could well provoke serious problems. Equally, Dr Holloway appreciated that I needed to begin engaging once more with the world.

A plan was hatched. We were going to slip away somewhere unnoticed and anonymously. We needed to be guaranteed privacy, and a safe place from which I could walk slowly and carefully back into the world. Mindy had found such a place. And we were going in a couple of days.

I hated the secrecy. No one could know where we were going, not even friends. If it did get out and we had to return to hospital to hide, it would be terrible to find ourselves looking for someone to blame. We didn't want anyone to be lumbered with the responsibility of keeping a secret that might well get out anyway.

I was told that I would be going to bed as usual on the evening of the great escape and would then be woken early in the morning. I had to have my bag packed with the few belongings I needed and be ready to leave. I packed and re-packed my bag every day to make sure I would be ready.

Chapter 14

ESCAPE TO SCOTLAND

Richard's medication became less intense as the days passed. His balance improved, he spent less time in bed, and his physiotherapy sessions were increased to two per day. The physios concentrated on pilates and aerobic exercise, together with relaxation techniques. They were a great team, concentrating on small achievements, and helping him to regain his strength.

Once the sessions increased, and with them his core strength and stability, he regained not only physical strength but also a more positive outlook. Richard had always waxed lyrical about the endorphin buzz he enjoyed when exercising. If ever he was down, I'd encourage him to visit the gym or go out for a run. He invariably returned recharged and happy. I sensed he wasn't yet experiencing the buzz, but at least his body was starting to perform again. And because he was more mobile, daily injections could cease. Anticlotting jabs in his stomach had left a chain of painful bruises. They wouldn't be missed.

Discussions with Rick Nelson had demonstrated Richard's 'increased insight' into his condition. This better understanding of his situation, what had happened to him and how he was improving, was a very positive sign. John Holloway, the medical director of the local Brain Injury Rehabilitation Centre at Frenchay, who took over

Richard's care, was very considered. Before a sentence left his lips you could sense the thought involved in the order of words, how they were delivered, how they'd be received. But whenever he spoke to Richard he was careful not to patronise or insult the intelligence hidden deep within the man in front of him. He was an expert.

Richard instantly warmed to him, and quickly turned off his usual act. John was very adept at gently cutting through the crap and discussing the real issues. His honesty was encouraging. He gave Richard enough information to convey the severity of his injury without causing alarm. Just enough so his advice would be taken seriously. I listened and watched the exchanges between them with enormous relief. Richard would be guided by him. In fact, John would help us for a great many months. He was accessible night and day, and became an invaluable guide through the most difficult stages of recovery.

Every journey I took was met by a small group of photographers at the entrance. They were respectful, and didn't attempt to gain entry to the hospital; and the photographers at home weren't intrusive, they were just waiting to see if Richard emerged. However, I was becoming a little nervous about the press. We were out of our depth with all the media coverage. Preoccupied as I was with keeping Richard happy, making sure everything was OK at home, updating his work colleagues, friends and family, and consulting with the medical team, I had no time left to make sure the press were correctly informed, and that worried me. Richard's agent had been approached by various publications that were very interested in his story, and I had no idea what to do. Luckily I was put in contact with someone who did. Gary Farrow, a highly respected PR professional, became an important part of our lives. Initially he was there to take care of media issues, but his role changed dramatically as Richard's condition improved.

Meanwhile, Richard was going stir crazy. He really wanted out, and was starting to get angry; to keep him in hospital for much longer would become counter-productive. But the issue was how to get him out of hospital without massive press attention. The flashing lights from a bank of press photographers could quite possibly put him at risk of a seizure or epileptic fit. Then there was the attention we'd be in for when word spread he was at home. Our house abutted a country lane; the press could literally lean over the gate and at one point see straight into the house.

The doctors were concerned Richard should enjoy freedom on his release from hospital, not feel like a prisoner in his own home. They suggested I try to get him away for a while, but the question was where? And how? The doctors were keen for Richard to go somewhere quiet where he could relax. Their one condition was that he shouldn't go on any long-haul flights. Gary and I discussed Ireland, but it was too complicated. The Lake District was too busy. Nowhere had the privacy he needed. Then we hit upon the solution: Scotland. A cottage in the Highlands. Perfect!

But it had to be done very carefully. No one, not even Richard, could know the plan we were hatching. If anything reached the ears of the press, it would be all over. They'd know he was coming out and he'd never manage to hide away. Gary arranged for a group of ex-special forces men to go into action on our behalf. They were great guys and professional to the last. I knew they'd make it happen.

Operation Joystick went into action. The brief we worked from went like this:

A multi-phase operation to enable the subject and his family to go on holiday for a week without the press becoming aware of the plans or their location during that time.

To minimise the number of people involved and the chances of being seen by third parties, we plan to move the family and the subject independently to a rendezvous point from where they will be driven in a large Winnebago to the ultimate destination.

One person to fly ahead, hire a car to recce the location and act as a ferry vehicle in case the Winnebago cannot drive right to the final destination.

Constant radio communication to be maintained at all times.

It was so difficult to keep the whole thing secret from Richard. He was incredibly excitable and would absolutely tell everyone he was getting out if even a whiff of it reached him.

I had to be at home on Friday evening. Ela was leaving us. She'd extended her stay by two weeks to help us out but had to return to university in Poland. Richard understood that I needed to say my goodbyes to her, and naturally would have to remain with the girls once she'd gone. But he'd expect me to take the girls to visit him on Saturday, which was impossible, as the team had to come to our house to finalise plans for our departure on Sunday night. So, against all advice, I told him we were leaving in the early hours of Monday morning. I made him swear to keep the secret, and explained the reasons why. He was excited, but he understood.

I called Richard's mum and told her we must 'disappear for a bit'. I asked her to buy a pay-as-you-go mobile phone and give me the number. I'd do the same. We would contact each other on the 'secret' phones.

Richard's brother Andy was due to visit him on Sunday afternoon. The visit would hopefully keep Richard's mind off imminent events, and make for an enjoyable afternoon.

Saturday

The two men in charge of the operation came to our house in Gloucestershire. They were accompanied by others in vehicles who were doing a sweep of the land surrounding the house. Some members of the press had been camping in the woods opposite in full camouflage gear with long lenses focused and ready for any interesting movement. There were plenty of hiding places, and these guys planned to identify their whereabouts in readiness for Sunday.

On their approach to our house in Gloucestershire they phoned me and I greeted them like friends at the door, as agreed. We chatted amiably in the kitchen over a couple of cups of tea and discussed the finer details of the plan.

Sunday

In the afternoon the daughter of one of the guys arrived. She was about eighteen years old, and was there to get to know the girls. She was to play an important role the following evening. She played with them for hours, and when she left she promised to see them again soon.

I stocked the house with dog, cat and pony food; wrote notes to neighbours who'd be looking after the place, and started to assemble luggage while the girls were playing in the garden.

On Sunday night I put the girls to bed as usual, then started running up and down stairs collecting everything and packing bags and suitcases. The team was already in position around the house; they'd ensured no one was watching. Simultaneously, other members of the team were sweeping the area surrounding the hospital in Bristol.

At eleven p.m. the guys returned and reversed their 4×4 so the back door of the vehicle practically opened into our hallway. There was a pile of luggage at the door. Once the luggage was in, the young girl who'd visited earlier helped me to wake Izzy and Willow.

'We're going on holiday,' I told them.

They were sleepy, but happy. They were secured in their child-seats before Captain, our Jack Russell, and Top Gear Dog joined them, to giggles of delight. While we were gone the other dogs would be looked after by the trusted friends and neighbours who generously offered their help.

I explained to the girls that I was going to fetch Daddy and meet them in a bit. They didn't once worry or question anything. There was nothing but smiles and laughter as they set off on their adventure, and great excitement at the prospect of getting Daddy back.

I jumped into the second car and followed them down to the motorway where they headed north to a motorway services and a waiting Winnebago. We were going south to the hospital in Bristol.

Fifteen minutes before our arrival, I called the duty nurse as arranged and told her our ETA.

'That's fine,' she said. 'I've just checked on him and he's fast asleep. 'you want me to go and wake him?'

'No thanks, it's OK, we'll get him up.'

Richard knew very well what time he was being sprung, and I was convinced there was no way he was asleep.

———————

This was better than Christmas when I was five. In a few hours, I would leave the hospital and go out into the world for what felt like the very first time. Lying on my back in the hospital bed, I was quivering with excitement, trying to control my breathing. My brother Andy had been in to see me that day. The visit was fun. He indulged me by playing with Lego, and we spoke about what was to come. I told him, in secret, that we were going away tomorrow and that no one, not even most of the hospital staff, knew about it. I spoke conspiratorially about our plans, about how we didn't want to fly anywhere because I might be spotted in an airport and because the doctors didn't want me to leave the mainland.

I trust him and every one of my friends and family entirely, and I knew that not one of them would even consider betraying a confidence at such a critical stage. In the end, it was enough for all of them to know that we would be safe, that we were going on the advice of the doctors, and that help was on hand if we needed it while we were away. I would later wish I had simply told them where we were going and explained that we wouldn't blame them if it ever got out. But the doctors had decreed that we absolutely must keep it secret. The conspiracy didn't help with my burgeoning paranoia.

When the knock at the door finally came, it didn't have to rouse me from sleep. I lay awake, still clutching the sheets, tensed like a ski-jumper at the top of the ramp. Desperate not to appear too keen and childish, I resisted the temptation to leap from the bed.

'Is it time, then?'

'Yes, let's go.'

The lights were dim and the corridor wall opposite loomed dark and blank. I had stuffed my treasured Lego sets into the holdall along with as many clothes as I could fit in. There was nothing else to take. We stepped out into the corridor and I felt the grip of nerves on my stomach. The night-time silence of the hospital was profound. This felt like somewhere between a scene from an action movie and leaving early on a family holiday as a child. I half expected my father to arrive, point at his watch and ask if we had packed everything in the car with the tents.

Mindy held my hand, and we spoke in whispers.

'The kids OK?'

'Yes, they're waiting in the motorhome. We'll drive there in the car and transfer.'

The calm, dark-clad figure alongside me clearly knew the route exactly and he moved in a manner that suggested he was familiar with situations where taking a wrong turn down a corridor in a building at night might be more than a minor inconvenience.

We crossed a carpeted lobby between plate-glass walls. And we walked outside. The air hit me, wrapped about my face and blew through me. I wanted to yell and scream and run about. I didn't. The car waited by the entrance. The back door was held open for me. I breathed in some more of the cool night air and climbed in.

'The girls are all waiting for you, Richard. They're fine. And they've got a couple of the dogs with them too.'

I felt exhilarated. Every moment that passed was a big, important one. I tried to collect them and preserve them. I would never do this again and I wanted to remember it. Nevertheless, I was asleep in seconds in the car and woke only when it pulled up alongside the motorhome. I climbed out, and a man grabbed my bag, passing it up to the open door.

The girls were sitting inside on a sofa. TG and Captain were there too.

———

We arrived at the hospital just before two a.m. The night porter unlocked the side door and we made our way quickly into the lift, then out and along the corridor to Richard's room. The duty nurse smiled as we passed.

Richard's room was in darkness, apart from a dim reading lamp on the bedside table. A still form covered in blankets lay on the bed. For a second I wondered whether he had fallen asleep.

'Richard?' I called in a loud whisper.

He recognised my voice instantly and threw back the covers. He was dressed and ready, with an enormous grin on his face. In a moment he was on his feet and hugging me.

'God, I've missed you.'

I smiled back and shushed him before introducing him to his rescuer, who was already asking which bags to take.

I'd left a black hoodie and a pair of sunglasses in Richard's room on my last visit and, despite his protestations, he now wore them to leave the building. It was a few steps to the waiting car, then he had to keep his head well down as we drove out of Bristol. Once on the motorway he held me close and told me of his excitement and the game he'd played with the nurse who kept coming in to check on him. He'd pretended to snore whenever she entered the room.

By three a.m. we were at the Winnebago. The girls were jumping around and playing, so ecstatic to see their daddy.

————

Suddenly, the world was in colour once more. I was home with my girls. I clutched them both, held on to them. They were excited to show me around inside the van. They showed me a big bedroom at the back with a real bed in it. They showed me their bed, with its row of smart lockers overhead, and a place where TG insisted on sleeping. I felt Mindy watching us. She stood back and studied what happened as I re-engaged with my children. She had taken us through one phase of recovery and now we were entering another. I was tired, but too alive to sleep.

Mindy sat next to me on the sofa bed, and we cradled the girls' heads as they slept. TG curled up by their feet. We talked softly of our lives together, of how our experiences might change things. The doctors had reassured us that, though it would be long and difficult, I would recover properly and fully. Right now, that felt like a very long way off. I was in too fragile a state ever to imagine feeling normal again. But we agreed on one thing: given a chance to carry on with our lives together when it had looked as though that would not be possible, we would do our level best to make the most of it.

I needed to sleep now; the excitement was taking its toll. As the van rumbled on through the night, I knew that I had to try to relax my mind. I grew worried that the sudden rush of new experiences might prove too much. I was scared again. The doctors had described how seeing too many different stimuli might trigger convulsions. I sat still, closed my eyes, and waited for something to happen. I had no idea what it would feel like, an epileptic fit, and with every rise in emotion or remote physical sensation I imagined one was starting.

At the back of the van was a bedroom. The kids had been impressed with the full-size double bed, and I surveyed it now from the sliding doors that led into the cabin. There were windows at the head and side of it, and through the blinds the lights of the motorway pulsed and flashed. I turned around to stare back into the main cabin and saw a similar pulsing as the overhead motorway lighting flashed by. Mindy looked up from where she sat, still cradling the girls as they slept.

'Go to sleep, darling. You'll be fine.'

Being scared had become an almost constant state for me

over the weeks, but was made no more pleasant by its familiarity.

'Mind, I'm worried to death. They tell you that flashing lights can trigger epilepsy even if they're on the telly. If they can do that to normal people sitting at home, what about me now?'

It sounded petulant and ungrateful. Mindy had coordinated this entire escape with the doctor's approval, and now I was rejecting it as too dangerous. What did I know anyway?

'And if I sleep in there' – pointing to the bedroom behind me – 'the lights are flashing even more.'

'No, look, I'll close the curtains.'

Mindy rose carefully from her bunk so as not to disturb Izzy and Willow and squeezed past me into the bedroom. She reached across the bed and pulled the curtains together. The room was dim now, and Mindy looked at me through the gloom.

'You'll be fine. The doctors said you'll be OK. What you need now is some sleep. Remember, they told you that the risks increased the more tired you get. So sleep is the best thing. Come on.'

She pulled the bedcover back and stepped to the side to make room for me to walk into the room and fall on to the bed.

'I'm sorry, I'm just scared. To come this far and then to . . .'

I tailed off. Exhaustion was taking over now. I understood the need for sleep, that it could make all the difference in my recovery. I closed my eyes and Mindy padded out of the room.

But sleep would not come. I lay and waited for a seizure to start, tried to access the remote extremities of my body to see if I could detect any warning sensation that something unpleasant was about to occur. The axle of the van thumped heavily as it dealt with a ripple in the motorway surface. I was actively trying to sleep, straining to do so, but I knew it would not work. I threw the covers off and got up. Mindy came back in.

'I can't sleep. Too scared. I just don't think I should be doing this.'

'Do you want to go back?'

'No. God, no. But I just . . . Maybe we should go back. This is a stupid idea. For God's sake, they said no flashing lights, no sudden noises. Listen to it. When the camper goes over a bump there's a huge noise. You can hear it in here because you're right over the back wheels. I'm going to have a fit and then I'll be stuck with them for life and I'll lose my driving licence and we won't be able to earn a living and we'll be ruined. Why didn't you just book a flight? We could have flown off somewhere warm. Who the hell would have spotted me anyway? Who cares if some bloke off a car show who banged his head recently gets on a plane? This was the worst thing you could have done to me. Just leave me and I'll sit in here and stay awake. You go and get some sleep in there and I'll sit in here, awake.'

She stood there, gripping the edge of the door. I was attacking her, blaming her for everything. The doctors had warned that patients recovering from head injuries can suffer problems with anger. Maybe this was what was happening now. We both knew it, and the knowledge made me angrier. I wasn't cross because of the bang on my head, I was cross because everyone wanted to kill me; to make me mad; to ruin all the hard work I had done in making myself better. It was all going to go wrong, and it was just because people didn't think.

'Darling, get some sleep. Please.'

Her voice was soft and warm as she placated me quietly. I lay on the bed, pulled the cover over my head to block out the lights and waited again to be gripped by a seizure. I wondered what it would feel like. Would Mindy know, or would I just seize up and die?

The road rumbled past below the bed as we travelled further from one world into another.

―――――

The girls had fallen asleep. They looked beautiful, cuddled up together on the enormous bed in the living area, a couple of blankets over them, and TG – who on every other car journey was sick – lying in front of their feet, edging them into the safest corner of the bed. She took on the role of a nanny dog from the moment the journey started.

My brief moment of peace was soon over. Richard couldn't settle in the bedroom; he was petrified he might suffer a seizure. I tried to reassure him. There was very little light coming through the windows – it was one-way security glass covered by blinds, which were covered by curtains – but that didn't matter. I understood enough about Richard's condition to know that reasoning with him was not the answer. Eventually he returned to the bed and pulled the covers over his head.

As I left the room, I realised he'd broken the sliding door off its runners. I tried to fix it back on, but it was quite heavy, and he heard me and grew angry. I wouldn't be able to fix it, and I needed to stay close to him. I couldn't join him in the bed; the door would slam. I had only one option. I put my hand between the door and its closing point and leant up against the wall at right angles to it, my right foot braced up against the opposite side of the Winnebago to avoid sliding down if I fell asleep. I stayed there through the night, sometimes grappling with the door when it escaped my grasp on a sharp bend, other times wincing as it trapped my fingers on a right-hand turn. When dawn came there was no respite. I couldn't leave my post until Richard woke up, and I had no intention of waking him. At least the scenery became visible, with the promise of a sunny day.

We were all together, a family again. Richard had been nervous the previous night, but that was understandable. The external stimuli had suddenly overwhelmed him, but he'd overcome it. He'd be OK. I yearned to climb into the bed next to him, to hold him and reassure him, but he needed as much rest as possible. The best I could do for him now was to remain there, with my crumpled fingers in the door.

———

I woke to find that the van was still ploughing on, but the light of day had ended the flash of passing streetlamps. The terrors of the evening were gone. Mindy was standing outside my door looking tired, but she kissed me good morning when I peered into the main cabin.

'Morning, darling. You finally got some sleep, then?'

Despite last night, she sounded warm. I knew how much she cared.

'Yes. Thank you. Sorry about shouting. I was scared.' I hung my head like a scolded schoolboy.

'I know. It's fine.'

'Where are we?'

'We're in Scotland. The guys have done brilliantly.' She motioned towards the two drivers up at the front.

'Oh yes. Morning, lads. All quiet, then?'

They muttered that yes, all was good.

On either side of the road ahead, the land swept back and grew to become gentle rolling hills. Beyond, lining the edge of the horizon to our right, were mountains, huge and green against the pale blue sky.

'What time is it?' I asked, even though I still wore my watch on my wrist. Asking the time made me more involved, more of a participant than a spectator.

'It's only nine, darling. You slept for four hours though.'

'Good. What time will we get there?'

'The guys reckon by four thirty. Depends on the traffic. You hungry?'

'What have we got?'

'We can stop. We can get whatever you want.'

Suddenly I felt gripped by a new worry. I didn't want to see anyone. I just didn't want to see strangers; I was scared of them. The idea of meeting people I didn't know made my stomach churn. I didn't even want to have two strange guys driving the truck. I was terrified of anyone I didn't know. Mindy must have seen the fear on my face.

'Darling, we can pull over at the services and park out of the way. We've got to stop anyway to let the dogs have a pee. You can stay in here and the guys will get us whatever you want. How would you like a bacon sandwich?'

I wasn't hungry; the thought of meeting strangers had killed my appetite. But I wanted a bacon sandwich at the service station because that's the sort of thing you did, out in the real world.

'Yes please, I'd love one. Let's do it, let's pull over.'

After a while, we drew up in a large car park and I hid in the bedroom. Peering under the curtain, I saw car wheels parked around the place. I shuddered and felt the tension through my shoulders. Mindy gave TG and Captain over to one of our chaperones and they took them outside. I couldn't imagine just striding down the steps like that, taking it all in and being taken in by other people. By strangers. I pressed myself into the gloom at the back of the bedroom. This was an important step, doing something because we had to. I had a job list again. And I ran away from it.

———

We all ate a 'full Scottish' breakfast, or at least we all ate a bit of it. Richard was visibly on edge at being stationary. The girls were running about and getting restless and I noticed Richard closing his eyes against their high-pitched voices on a couple of occasions. This was difficult for him. He'd been living in a different world since the crash and had been dropped back into the bedlam of a young family.

I asked him if he'd like to go back into the bedroom and lie down, but he was adamant: 'I've done enough lying down to last me a lifetime. I want to be here with you and the girls.'

'OK, but don't overdo it, will you?'

I joined him on the sofa and put my arm around him where he sat with Willow on his lap. Izzy was happy with her colouring book, the dogs at peace on the floor, as if knowing instinctively the world needed to hush a while, to give Richard time to acclimatise.

As we moved off on the final leg of the journey, Richard was careful not to look out of the windows for longer than a few seconds at a time. His brain couldn't cope with the complexities of the view. It was far easier for him to avoid looking. Whenever the Winnebago slowed down, he'd enjoy admiring the view again, and point out interesting things to the girls. We saw streams babbling and chasing as they cut their way through mountainsides, powerful rivers flowing majestically through the valleys, the thickest of forests, standing tall and proud on the hillsides, and there, in the distance, our destination: the Highlands.

Just after 4.15 we arrived at a five-bar gate. A young woman was there to greet us and lead the way in her car to the cottage we'd rented for three weeks. The Winnebago just made it along the narrow winding tracks. We turned a final corner and there it was, in a clearing surrounded by woodland – a staggeringly beautiful little house.

A Land Rover was standing outside. I'd ordered it to use as our transport and Richard was thrilled the second he saw it. We were escorted into the bright little house and Richard was instantly besotted. A roaring fire had been lit in the living room and mugs of steaming hot tea greeted us. The lads carried our bags inside. Richard excused himself and quickly disappeared into the master bedroom. He was exhausted. I was so proud of him. He was thrilled with the place; he was ready to relax. He just needed a bit of privacy.

Chapter 15

THE COTTAGE IN THE HIGHLANDS

I had never been to the cottage before, but there was a comforting familiarity to the place. The rooms were large but not overwhelming. Heavy curtains dressed every window. Underfoot, red carpets swirled contentedly as I padded from room to room. On every wall hung watercolours of the hills and forests that surrounded the cottage. This was a warm and friendly house, perfectly suited to a family wanting to spend time in a wonderful place and enjoy it to the full.

I was happy as I roamed about. We could be OK here; this felt like the safe place we needed in which to hide away and get better. And then I found the door. It was at the end of a corridor. It was not inherently sinister but it looked out of place. In the wall to the right of it was another door that opened on to the bathroom. But where did this one go?

Mindy was in the kitchen, rooting through the provisions. I asked her about the door. She explained patiently that we had been lucky enough to employ someone to cook for us once a day, so that we could have more time relaxing together as a family. The cook lived next door with her husband, and the door went through to her house.

I froze with fear. This safe, secure little place by the woods had a door in it that opened up into another house with strangers in.

I walked slowly back down the corridor to look through the window into the yard beyond. The walls around it were built of the same dark stone as the cottage and had grown darker still with the steady rain. Past the yard, the looming conifers braced themselves on the mountainside and dripped rain into the pine-needle carpet below. I could hear the rain hissing, and a slow wind shouldering through the trees. I looked back at the door. The friendly familiarity of the cottage had been replaced by my unfriendly but no less familiar companion: fear.

———

I'd called ahead a week before to order an enormous list of groceries. The kitchen cupboards were filled with goodies and I'd agreed a list of casseroles and pies which the cook would prepare and store in the freezer. From bitter experience, I knew holiday arrangements rarely went to plan, but this time we'd struck gold. Everything was as promised. The house was comfortable, clean and welcoming, and the children were outside with the dogs, running around and playing, all exhilarated to be free. I watched them from the kitchen window as they ran and laughed, then their obvious excitement as they discovered two Highland ponies in the paddock. They both came running in to find me.

'Mummy! Mummy! Quick, come and look!' Willow cried, her cheeks flushed and eyes wide as she grabbed my hand and led me outside.

'Oh, Mummy,' said Izzy, 'they're so beautiful!'

'What are?' I pretended not to know their secret.

'Just wait, you won't believe it,' Izzy continued.

We rounded the corner from the front door and walked towards the side of the cottage.

'Oh, girls, aren't they gorgeous!'

The two heavy-set grey ponies nonchalantly looked over before slowly wandering towards us to say hello. They were big softies and allowed the children to stroke them through the fence. I left them there, talking to the two ponies, and returned to the kitchen to make a cup of tea. Watching the scene through the window, I was moved to tears. To me, that was all we needed, two little girls lost in the joy of ponies. Simple pleasures. If only everything could be so simple.

Richard appeared at my shoulder, and put his arm around my waist.

'Well done, Mind.' He smiled. 'This place is fantastic.'

I sighed. 'I'm glad you like it. I was worried you might not.'

'I know I'm difficult to please, but you've done us proud.'

He sounded calm, but I sensed an air of unease. I didn't pursue it. He sipped his tea and glanced out of the window.

'Oh, wow, look at the girls! Aah, look at them!'

They were still talking to the ponies, but now Willow was on her haunches, her hands between her knees, deep in conversation with her pony, while Izzy leaned against the fence, stroking the mane of the other. We stood there and watched them for a few minutes, until they noticed us and the biscuits we were eating and ran inside.

—————

Breakfast would be enormous; it always was. Each morning we were presented with thick bacon and chubby sausages with mushrooms, tomatoes and beans. I would wolf it down, my appetite returning fast.

I lay in bed and listened to the sizzles and splashes from the kitchen. Mindy must be in the kitchen too, because the bed beside me lay empty. I could hear that the girls were up: giggles came through the door, though the girls themselves did not. They were still cautious around me, aware that the usual rough and tumble of our lives together had to be put on hold for a while. Daddy was poorly. They understood this and were humouring me and giving me space.

Mindy had brought a few shirts and pairs of jeans and hung them in the wardrobe that stood next to the window. I looked at it and considered how much better it was to be in charge of my own life again. I could get up and dress myself now, even choosing the clothes I wore and what I did with my time afterwards. I pulled on jeans and a rough blue shirt and walked, barefoot, out of the bedroom and into the living room.

The girls were playing on the carpet in front of the fireplace. Lego pieces were scattered to every corner of the room. I had given them a set of their own to play with. The picture on the box depicted a garage with five cars to build. A man in a blue hat walked across the forecourt carrying a big spanner and the cars were customised with flames on them. I thought I'd had a similar set as a child, and I may have done. If not, I had certainly spent many hours building a similar scene. I was happy now that the girls wanted to do the same.

A fight broke out and interrupted my happy thoughts. Izzy was cross because Willow wanted to build the green car. She shouted and told her that she couldn't build it, that it was hers and Willow must build the white one. And why did she have to spoil everything? The noise of their shouts rose and my face grew tense. The argument turned into noisy bickering and the sound of it chattered and rattled about me.

'Come on, you can both play. Izzy, can you let Willow build

the green one? She'll give it back to you afterwards. Go on, she's only small and she doesn't understand.'

Izzy pushed the green pieces towards her sister. 'Go on then, Willow, you build it.'

'Say thank you, Willow.'

'Thank you.' She muttered it, but then looked up at her sister and smiled.

The argument was over. But it had left me drained. This was hard, looking after the kids. I felt closer to them than ever before, probably, but closer to them more as a contemporary than as a parent. I could happily have joined in and played their games all day, but to bear even a slight responsibility for them was very uncomfortable. I felt like I had when we first took Izzy home from hospital as a one-week-old baby. We walked in, sat down on the sofa cradling her tiny wrinkled form and waited for someone to come and tell us what to do. There were no instructions, no rulebook, and we realised that for the first time in our lives we were fully in charge. That feeling came back to haunt me now, and I felt dizzy with the pressure. I didn't want to be in charge, I wanted to play.

'Girls, let's all build it together. Here, I'll build the green one.'

The routine established itself. After breakfast we went for a 'whatever the weather' walk. This was a practice we had established years before: once a walk was elected upon, we would go whether it was raining or not. The kids loved it and were splashing along happily now as Mindy and I tailed them in our heavy Drizabones, rain slicking off them on to our boots and dripping from the brims of our wide hats on to our shoulders. It was wet but not too cold. Izzy wore a bright blue coat and

Willow a pink one. Their wellies were a riot of multi-coloured bees, flowers and frogs as they leapt and danced.

Mindy shouted, 'Girls, don't jump in the big puddles, please. You'll fall in and have to swim across.'

They giggled at their mother's crazy idea and grinned under their hoods, faces shiny with water and excitement. The rain was soft but insistent. It was, I declared, 'very wet' rain. Mindy laughed, and we held hands. Behind us, TG and Captain snouted along the edges of the patch, sniffing the hollows where sheep had slept and deer had chewed the grass.

'Where are we going?' Izzy's voice was strident and confident over the rain.

'To the picnic place, of course,' Mindy answered.

'Ooh, it's miles away.'

Izzy stopped as she moaned and I saw Willow tense as she prepared to join in.

'It's not far. It's just up there, past the bridge.'

'Yes, it's not far,' I chimed in, trying to help placate them. 'You've walked there before loads of times. Come on, race you.'

We set off, covering the last piece of open ground rising to the edge of the forest in short time. The girls ran as hard as they could and I splashed and staggered about in mock tiny steps to stay alongside them. We passed under the green, dripping canopy.

'Let's walk now,' Izzy said in the forest's silence, and she slipped her hand into mine. 'Come on, Willow, let's hold hands for the last bit.'

Willow grasped the fingers of my right hand. The dogs came past, Captain trotting merrily, TG barging into Willow as she overtook.

'TG! She hurt me, she pushed me.'

'Willow, you're fine, sweetie. She's just clumsy, that's all. Silly clumsy dog.'

I made fun of TG, sticking out my tongue, rolling my eyes and panting to make the girls laugh.

'She's really clumsy,' Willow giggled.

Our picnic place was a clearing on a bend of the path between the dark conifers. Logs on the ground made perfect seats, tables and climbing frames. We sat with our backs to the hill and looked out over the tops of the trees sloping away to the valley and our cottage. We would eat sandwiches, drink coffee from a flask, play games, make up stories and fill our time laughing and talking. When the girls wandered off, Mindy and I spoke about the future and the past.

———

Richard would confide his innermost feelings out there in the woods. The log where we sat at picnic times became his talking place.

'I've been really ill, haven't I? I'm still bad.'

'You've improved so much in such a short time. You should be proud of yourself.'

'I kept thinking there was nothing wrong with me, that I was a fraud, and everyone was being nice to me under false pretences. But they weren't. I know that now.'

He was so sad. Surrounded by all this beauty, yet he still felt so awful.

I'd packed his watercolours and pastels, sketching materials and pads. As I looked about us I was bombarded with a thousand different hues of green, incredible dappled sunlight piercing through the forest canopy and dancing off every rock. But Richard refused to paint. He even refused to take a photograph. He confided in me: 'I'm scared I'll get stuck where I was when I was at college. You know I hated those years. I want to get past that.'

I nodded. I understood.

At times, huge blocks of memory would just fall suddenly into his head. It was quite alarming for him. He'd explain that within a second an enormous gap was filled with years of experience in amazing detail.

If he didn't want to explore his artistic talents yet, that was fine.

———

That day's picnic was a good one. The girls had played happily and I lazed under the trees for a while thinking fondly of our family camping trips to the Forest of Dean when I was young. We had used an old blue ridge tent and sat happily for hours inside, the five of us cramped around a small table, playing cards as the rain hammered on to the canvas. Looking up through the trees over our Scottish picnic place, I remembered the walk down through the woods to the river in the Forest of Dean and the metal swing bridge that crossed it. The floor of the bridge was made of heavy wire mesh and you could look down past your feet to see the river as it passed beneath. As people made their way across, the bridge bucked and moved, which delighted my eight-year-old senses. I tried to swing the bridge deliberately. My tiny weight could make no impression on the thick metal cables that fixed the structure at each end, but I wondered if it would be possible one day to swing it so much that it completed a full circle, like a swing going over the top in a playground.

Now, in Scotland, nearly thirty years later, we finished our picnic and gathered our bags and our coats for the short walk back to the cottage. I looked at the girls in their colourful clothes and sturdy little boots and I felt happy.

As we approached the cottage, I saw a car, a small hatchback. I whirled into a state of paranoia and fear. I didn't worry that we were about to be attacked or robbed, I simply could not bear the idea of meeting strangers. It had become a phobia.

Our walks through the forest were great for the girls, and they served as a fantastic way to tire Willow enough for an afternoon nap, which I encouraged Richard to copy. He soon agreed, and his nap became as much a part of the routine as Willow's.

It was an essential part of my day too. While Richard slept I made telephone calls. I updated his parents, spoke with the doctors and ensured that everything at home and work was running smoothly. Every day there would be at least ten messages to be dealt with, most of which had to be done out of Richard's earshot. He was too eager to get involved with work issues, and in addition I was regularly in conversation with the doctors. I had to be completely honest with them about his condition.

On our return from a walk one afternoon we noticed a strange car parked outside the house. Richard became agitated and nervous. He refused to walk further than the woods until I'd investigated. The girls came with me and we meandered into the house. Straight away the smell of cooking reached my nostrils. The housekeeper/cook had turned up and was preparing our food for the following week. It was her car. Although she lived in the cottage next door, she'd just returned from a trip to the shops to pick up extra ingredients, and unloading was easier from outside our house. I went back out and motioned for Richard to join us. He was relieved when he heard who our visitor was, but his dislike of unpredictability was apparent. It occurred to me that the doctors' advice about structure and routine had been wisely enforced. As long as we stuck to routine and he knew how his day would unfold, it was OK; had we gone straight home, with the natural interruptions and opportunities for unexpected visitors, he would certainly have struggled to cope.

The following day it seemed ridiculously busy on our walk. We had to leave the track several times to let Land Rovers pass, and each time Richard would pull down his hat and walk with his back to them. There were many walkers on the footpaths too, which added pressure. It ruined the day for him, and he remained in a foul mood.

The only light relief came when we ate our supper, a casserole prepared by the cook. I immediately noticed it contained one ingredient Richard had always detested – celery. I was very nervous about even offering the meal to him, but to my amazement, not only did he devour it with relish, he asked for seconds.

But that evening he was quiet. I watched his expression as he fought unknown battles in his mind; it was easy to read on his face the internal distress. I was powerless to help. All I could do was offer support in whatever way he would take it. Later, he confided his hatred of the injury which afflicted him. We spoke long into the night and I reassured him that all would be well, but as I lay awake, for the first time I felt really sorry for myself. I had no one to share this with. There seemed to be no gentleness, no softness any more, just difficulty.

———

This was a moment to savour. I pulled the laces on my trainers and fastened them tightly.

'You won't overdo it?'

'No. I shall be sensible and moderate. Honest.'

Mindy, standing behind me in the hallway, smiled.

'Really? You'll be sensible? How long are you going to be?'

'About twenty minutes should do it.' I stretched my calf muscles as I spoke. 'I'll go up the hill towards the picnic place. Tell you what, I'll just run in that direction for ten minutes, turn round and run back.'

'Take care, baby.'

Turning round to face the open spaces in front of the cottage, I tugged my lightweight running jacket down a little and pinched the peak of my baseball cap between finger and thumb to adjust it.

'I'll be careful, don't worry.'

And I trotted off up the track towards the woods and the hills.

The sense of freedom was immense; I could go where I wanted. I was alone. Ahead, the forest waited, and the bridge and the corner, and any number of new things I was now allowed to wander among on my own. Running into the forest felt like an embrace as I passed under the thick-needled branches. Inside, the air was tangy and heavy with the scent of pine needles, damp undergrowth and peat. I heard the stream running down from the hilltops, crashing over the stones.

As I ran past the picnic place, I thrilled to the sensation of being just a bloke out for a run, passing a place he took the kids to for a picnic. It was normal. My legs strained as I crested the hill, but not so badly that I needed to slacken the pace. In fact, the slight pain felt good; I was pushing a little, making myself work for the first time in what felt like years.

The thrill now was building to euphoria. I measured my breathing against my paces and enjoyed the double beat as my chest reverberated to every footfall. The trees went past me faster. And I wondered what would happen if their flashing, flickering trunks acted as a sort of stroboscope and triggered a seizure. Would I collapse and die immediately? Or would I fall to the ground and lie alone in the damp verge to die slowly of exposure before a hillwalker stumbled across my grizzly remains? But I felt no fear at the prospect. Right now, I was running and it felt good. If it caused something bad, well, so be it.

As the endorphins released by the exercise flooded my system, my confidence rose. I laughed out loud, swung my arms wildly over my head and took a path that dropped off to the right into the muddy woods. Ahead lay a wooden fence in which, straddling the path, was a wooden gate. I swung the gate open and closed it carefully behind me before I carried on, pumping my legs to take me over the rise where the fence line lay, and then to follow the path that dropped down through the trees towards a small valley.

As I ran, my thoughts grew calmer. This was what I needed; this would help more than anything else. Just one tiny thought floated in to disturb my new-found calm: had I closed the gate? Well, yes, I remembered carefully latching the metal clasp. I had made sure it was properly closed, just as I have closed tens of thousands of other gates on other runs. But I didn't trust my memory. Had I really closed it, or was I imagining it?

And then another thought arrived: was this paranoia? The

doctors had warned that paranoia might rear its head, along with compulsive behaviour patterns. Was this burning desire to run back up a substantial muddy hill to check a gate that I knew for a fact I had closed only minutes earlier compulsive behaviour? Was I being paranoid about my compulsion? I turned round and set off back up the hill. If it's going to send me mad worrying about it, I thought, I'll go and check the gate anyway.

I ran back up the hill. The gate stood firmly closed. I felt broken and shamed.

Richard had been too long on his run. He'd promised to be back within twenty minutes. Thirty had passed, and I was worried. I was sure he'd overdone it and was lying in pain somewhere, or had got lost, which was actually even more of a worry as it was starting to get dark.

I told the girls to get their coats and wellies on, we were going for a drive in the Land Rover. They were pleased and had just started to argue over who would sit in the front when the cottage door opened and a sweaty, muddy Richard stood in the doorway.

'Did you have a good run?' I started to take my coat off as I spoke.

'It was OK. Where are you off to?'

'I was about to come and look for you. You were quite a while and I was getting a bit worried.'

Richard recounted the episode with the gate, concerned that he was chronically paranoid.

'I couldn't begin to tell you the number of times I do stuff like that,' I said. 'Rechecking something I absolutely know I've already done. It's just like the lost key syndrome. Every time you've lost your keys in the past you haven't instantly assumed you've got permanent brain-damage. You just had to check the gate. Simple.'

He seemed a little appeased, and went off for a shower. Meanwhile I had to take the girls round the block because I'd promised them a ride in the Land Rover.

———

Sitting on a bench to take in a view and daydream is not something I do by accident. As I lowered myself on to the wooden slats of the bench to the front of the cottage, I looked across to the forest-clad mountains under a grey, leaden sky and readied myself for a relaxing, thoughtful pause. Mindy and the girls were busy inside the cottage and I had stolen outside to take stock on my own and let my mind wander.

I breathed in slowly and relaxed my mind, ready to let my thoughts wander where they would. And nothing happened. I gazed at the mountains and the forest. I let my eyes de-focus and blur the image to a tinted smudge. I couldn't daydream. I thought about where we were, what we were doing, why we were there. I thought about what might be happening elsewhere in the world, who else might have sat on this bench and looked at the same scene. But my thoughts wouldn't wander. Like a faithful but irritating dog, they kept returning to my heel to look up and ask for direction.

I looked at the tree in front of me. I knew that it had roots that ran into the ground and brought moisture and nutrients up the trunk. I knew that the leaves spread to capture the energy of the sun and that their greenness facilitated the photo-synthesis that brought the thing to life. But there was no poetry, nothing fantastic or mystical about the tree. I could remember previous encounters with trees – my memory was working now. I recalled carving names into their sturdy hearts, perched high above a woodland floor. I could remember climbing until I thought I would fall through thin branches for ever. I remembered the huge arms of the beech trees in the Chiltern hills around my old home in Buckinghamshire. The beeches were the patriarchs of the woodlands, and they grew to dominate by starving all others of light. I remembered sitting on a beech branch as thick as a cow, and being moved by it. But I could not be moved now. I could grasp facts, remember fanciful thoughts, but I could make no more to add to those that had come and gone before. I could not daydream. The thought of it took hold of my mind and, like the dominating beech trees, shaded every other thought out of existence. I felt thinner, made less, because of the loss of this simple act. I could not daydream, and maybe I never would be able to again.

––––––

The evenings in Scotland were my most feared part of the day. I'm not sure whether it was fatigue or boredom, but often Richard would be in a bad mood. He couldn't watch any television, because even the slightest hint of confrontation and he'd have to leave the room. Instead, we spent evenings playing Top Trumps, or leafing through car magazines.

Once the girls were in bed we whiled away an hour before climbing into bed ourselves. We were both exhausted. Richard could lie in late every morning before he joined the girls and me in the kitchen.

We were at the breakfast table one morning when he suddenly stopped eating and sat bolt upright. His face contorted into so many different expressions it was really very strange to watch.

'You OK? What's up?'

I watched his face change involuntarily. He looked different. He didn't look like Richard. His face was ashen and instantly aged ten years. Had I seen this man in the street I wouldn't have recognised him. It was frightening. I sat paralysed, hypnotised by this uncontrollable force, waiting for it to stop.

When it ceased, moments later, he was left bewildered and confused. All I could do was hug him. Richard explained that as he'd sat there, from nowhere about ten different emotions hit him all at once. He was bombarded by them from deep within his psyche.

I felt we were being reminded that it was going to be difficult. Very difficult. But we'd get through it.

———

Someone was out there. I was sure of it. I leaned round to look outside. The rough track that ran in front of the cottage disappeared to my right. But I saw no one. Izzy and Willow played happily on the carpet behind me. They were colouring in; their pencils and felt-tip pens lay scattered in front of the fireplace. I had heard a car drawing up and had leapt from the floor where I sat with them. My motivation had come from a desire to protect them, and to hide from whoever was approaching. What would I do if they came to the door?

'What is it, Daddy?'

'Oh, just the rain. Just looking at the rain.'

I saw a van emerge from the bend in the track to the right and my shoulders froze. It was dark green and old. I slid further away from the window to hide behind the wall, leaving just enough room for my right eye to watch as the van rolled in front of the cottage. It stopped. The door opened. I crouched now, hiding below the window sill.

'What are you doing, Daddy?'

'I'm just seeing what's out there.'

My heart raced now. I suddenly felt angry. How could Mindy have left me alone? I didn't feel ready for the responsibility of looking after the kids on my own.

I watched the shape of the driver moving around the front of the van. I was too scared to look directly at him. He might see me. Through the blurry bottom edges of the window I could make out the shape of him in dark green clothes walking towards the front door. If he thought there was nobody in, he would go away. And then the letterbox clattered. It felt like a direct invasion. Then I reasoned, if he was leaving a letter, it meant he was going away. I stayed hidden but breathed out and felt my shoulders sag. But I was angry still – angry that I'd been left alone, angry that I was scared, angry that I was hiding under the window sill. I was just angry.

Izzy and Willow were still playing by the fireplace. I shuffled over to them.

'How's it going, girls? Let's have a look.'

As the girls showed me their colouring and chatted about what they had done, my anger faded to sadness.

———

Our grocery stock began to dwindle midway through the second week, and there was only one way to get more supplies. I'd have to go out and buy them. I could take the girls with me; they'd enjoy it.

Richard disagreed. 'Don't be silly, I'll look after the girls. You go shopping, have a break.'

He was trying to sound matter-of-fact, but it was very unconvincing.

I knew the way to the nearby village, and calculated it would take twenty minutes to get there, the same on the return journey, and twenty minutes to shop. I could be back in an hour. I was concerned about leaving Richard, but the girls are very sensible for their ages, and I was sure they'd try hard to be good for him. He wasn't taking no for an answer anyway, and if I stayed and debated the issue he'd just get very angry. He promised to go next door and call the cook if he had any problems.

I prepped the girls. 'You can have your favourite tea tonight if you're good for Daddy. That means no shouting or squealing, no arguing, and all toys away before teatime, OK?'

I jumped into the Land Rover, waved goodbye to them all as I drove past the sitting-room window, and worried myself half to death over the next fifty-seven minutes.

On my return I was relieved to find them all happily playing with Lego in the living room. However, Richard could bear no more, and as soon as he saw me he escaped into the bedroom. I took him the customary cup of tea.

'How was it?'

'Oh, Mind . . .' His voice was shaky as he cradled the mug in his hands; he seemed fragile. 'It's scary being on my own with them now, being responsible.' He paused, sensing my concern. 'But it was fine, honestly. We had a lovely time. I'm just tired.'

'I shouldn't have gone.' The trip had caused him unnecessary stress, I felt terrible.

'No, Mind, I'm their father. I just need to get used to it, that's all.'

He was disappointed. He adored the girls, was always fantastic with them, but he'd been brutally reminded of his new limitations.

'Get into bed and have a nap. I'll wake you in a couple of hours.

You're doing really well, you know. I mean *really* well.'

'I know, but it doesn't feel like it. I hate being like this.'

I cuddled up to him on the bed.

'You get better every day. We'll get through this, y'know?'

'We will, won't we?' There was doubt in his voice.

'Oh, yes. We'll come back the new, improved, stronger us. The same as before, only more so.'

'God, I love you.'

'I love you too.'

I kissed him.

'Now, get some sleep.'

Outside, the light was fading, but just as dusk approached I saw through the hall window, no more than eighty feet away in the evening mist, a large stag. We'd heard them roar every night, but we'd seen nothing this close. I wanted to wake Richard, to share the moment with him, but he was asleep and to wake him would be selfish. I found the girls though, and the three of us sat by the window and watched that magnificent creature for some minutes before he disappeared into the mist.

Chapter 16

GOING HOME

We were going home tomorrow. Mindy had made the arrangements; a car would pick us up and drive us all home. We had packed our bags and they lay scattered about the cottage. I wanted to go out for one last run. Izzy and Willow were sprinting up and down the corridor by the kitchen and Mindy was preparing their tea. Crouched by the front door, I pushed my feet into my trainers, tying the laces quickly.

Leaning against the wall to stretch my legs, I looked across at the dark oak coat-stand. Still hanging from it were our long Drizabone waterproofs and the girls' coats. Gathered under it were our walking boots. This place had been everything we needed. We had enjoyed peace, tranquillity and a chance to regroup as a family. But I had also learned more about how I had damaged myself. As every day passed, I looked back and realised how unwell I had still been that day and how much better I now was. And then another day would pass. But now was not the time to slope about fretting. I was going for my final run through the beautiful wooded Highlands and I was determined to savour it.

The letterbox rattled as the door shut behind me. I turned right, ran the length of the rough road in front of the house and felt the surface soften as the road gave way to a track. To my left, the rough grass lay flat and still. Beyond it, a fringe of trees climbed the mountainsides in the distance. In front of me, the forest stood familiar and inviting.

My legs felt stronger now; I was running every day and feeling the benefit. I reached out in longer strides until I passed under the first few trees and into the forest. Crossing the footbridge, I smiled at the sound of the stream, now a small river, dashing underneath. I leaned to the left as I turned to run past the picnic place. I would miss our time there together as a family and the hours that Mindy and I had spent holding hands on an old log – two people who love each other talking over an experience that nearly parted them for ever, and making plans for the future. We had looked forward as well as back across our time together and had become the stronger for it.

I pressed on, cresting the hill and running down again, along a wide and muddy path bordered by conifers. The path reached the bottom of a shallow valley and curved to the right. I followed it round, enjoying the feeling that I was running well, all systems functioning at optimum level. I had worked hard to get my fitness back; it mattered to me a lot. This was something I could do for myself, something I could be proud of achieving, and that pride mattered more than the achievement itself.

I was running across the hillside now on a track that followed the contours roughly but dipped gently to descend through the trees. To my right, the forest stood dense and busy until it gave way to a clearing that opened back from the track for a hundred metres or so. I saw how a few straggly bits of undergrowth had taken advantage of the thin sunlight to form a fringe. And emerging from the edge of the trees to walk confidently into the clearing was a stag. It moved slowly, but not from caution.

Its antlered head turned to scan the ground in front and to either side.

It saw me, or caught my scent, and stopped. From where I stood I could see curves of muscle stretching across its brown flanks and forming its shape. I could see the awkward joints of its hips and the strength of its legs tapering down to slender points. And I could see its deep brown eyes swivelling below the woody turrets of its antler crown.

Around us the forest paused, frozen. The shooting season had ended several days ago and the local gamekeepers believed that the deer knew, to the day, when this happened and grew braver and less cautious. In front of me now, the stag surveyed this interloper in his forest kingdom, and I felt its confusion. I was smaller, slower and without the spiked antlers that weighed on its head to signify rank, status and potency. It turned away, then turned to face me once more. I breathed slowly, a privileged observer. It turned for a final time and walked slowly back into the forest, breaking into a trot as it reached the trees.

I stayed where I was for some time. My moment had found me, a moment I knew would stay with me for ever. I felt blessed and lucky as I broke into an easy trot back to the cottage and my family.

———

I took a five-minute drive in the Land Rover the day before we left Scotland; I needed to top up the fuel and it was an opportunity to savour my last memories of that amazing place. I drove across the hillside and through the forests, drinking in every last detail – the enormous pine trees which reached far into the sky, the colours of the heathers, the magic of the tiny red squirrels as they darted across the road in front of me, and the grace and majesty of those beautiful deer. I was suddenly overcome by a desperate longing to stay. I burst into tears and had to pull over. I didn't want to go back, didn't want to leave this wonderful place, didn't want to face the complications of our life at home. It was peaceful here; safe, friendly. I wished life were different, but I knew that was impossible. There was no point in running away; we had to face our demons and overcome them. Even so, the short drive back to the house, saying farewell to the place that had become our sanctuary, was one of the saddest journeys I've ever known.

The car arrived to take us home just after lunch. We'd calculated to arrive home around midnight. There wouldn't be any press around at that time of night and hopefully we could walk straight in. The girls said goodbye to the ponies and clambered into their seats. Richard and I thanked the cook and her husband for looking after us and joined them in the car.

It seemed to take an awful lot longer getting home, and we stopped for a burger at teatime. The driver parked in the corner of the motorway services car park, and I fetched a large selection of fast food. None of us was particularly thrilled at going home – even the dogs had acclimatised – but as we reached the outskirts of Gloucestershire we all started to pick up. For the girls, it was returning to their rooms and teddies, and their faithful pets. For me, it was the familiarity of my home, and knowing that when Richard crossed the threshold the picture, finally, could start to get back to normal.

I watched him as he sipped his tea, slumped on the oversized sofa in the sitting room, his hair dishevelled, and a strange beard-like thing on his chin. I loved him so very much. I was so grateful he was alive, so proud to be home together, shoulder to shoulder, ready to carry on.

———

This didn't feel the same as a homecoming after a long holiday. I felt a gentle surge of warmth and excitement at crossing the threshold, but something was different. I had been away for just five weeks. The house had not changed; everything looked the same. The dogs gave me their customary welcome, bounding around and barking happily. TG and Captain had melded straight back into the pack and assumed their places. I walked from room to room, standing in each one and taking it in.

I slept deeply that night. The next morning I stood at the top of the stairs and listened as Izzy and Willow dashed about, picking up favourite toys and saying hello to the cats. From the landing I could see the painting of a horse that I bought Mindy for Christmas two years ago. I looked down past the stairs and studied the wooden trunk we picked up from a junk shop to keep our boots tucked tidily away. Behind the trunk, wedged in a corner, stood the wooden staff I collected on a walking trip across the Lake District twenty years ago. I was surrounded by memories. It should have been comforting.

Drifting back down the stairs, I stopped as Crusoe, our Border collie, walked up to me and pressed her head against my hip. I stroked her neck and felt her bunched muscles, straining to contain the energy and excitement as she resisted leaping on me and barking. Crusoe ran off to reunite once more with TG and Captain, her feet scrabbling noisily for grip on the wooden floor, and I walked into the dining room.

Mindy was elsewhere in the house now and I knew that I should be helping unpack our bags. But something was still wrong. Why did this not feel like the joyous homecoming I had dreamed of nearly every waking hour in hospital? I rested my hand on the polished surface of the table and looked at the bookcase standing at the far wall. My eyes wandered across the titles. There were books from my childhood, art reference books from college, novels read and re-read over decades, and books bought recently, just before the crash. The dogs were outside now and their happy barks and yelps came across the lawn beyond the windows. I remembered Sunday roasts with the girls; I remembered parties late into the night round this very table.

And I realised that I felt sad. Finally, I had made it home, back to my own hearth. Despite the pain and the confusion, I was back. The doctors had said it might take me years to get home, but I had done it in just a few weeks. Yet now, standing here in my own house with my family and dogs around me, I felt sad. I was, for the first time, in a familiar environment, one that was familiar to me from a time before the crash. I had lived in this house; laughed, shouted, argued and played. In flashes I remembered hundreds of little incidents with incredible clarity. I saw friends, heard laughter, remembered the quiet, private moments. And I knew why I felt sad. This was the first time I had been somewhere I could remember being before I damaged my brain. This was the first time I had met myself. And I knew that though the house was the same, I would never be the same again. Everything that had gone on in this house before would feel different if I went through it again now. My reactions would be different, my interpretation of it different. The home was familiar, but I was a stranger. There was a huge distance between me and this life that I had led. Everything was the same – everything except me. The sameness in the things around me just served to illuminate the strangeness in me.

I found Mindy and we held each other. I didn't need to tell

her that I was sad, or why. She knew. We had made it this far
and we were sure as hell going to carry on.

'You OK?' She spoke softly, her head on my shoulder.

'Yes. Just feels a bit ... weird, that's all.'

'I know.'

'Where are the girls?'

'Putting their boots on. We're going outside to say hello to
the pony.'

'Come on then. I'd like to do that too.'

'You sure you're OK?'

'Yeah. I'll be fine.'

AFTERWORD

It's now over a year since I sat on a bench in Scotland and wept when I realised I could not daydream any more. I can daydream now; my mind wanders and roams as freely as ever it did, maybe more so. I'm no longer terrified of strangers and I can get through a day without needing a nap. My emotions remained tricky for a while; I was at the whim of whatever particular powerful emotion struck me at any time, often for no discernible reason. Sometimes, though, I could recognise these phantom emotions for what they were, and even trace their route into my head.

I wandered across my garden some months ago and saw, from the corner of my eye, my old battered Land Rover. I must have thought to myself how much I loved that old thing because seconds later I was overwhelmed with a great flood of love, charging up through my chest to dominate everything, just as it does when I think about my daughters. I had, briefly, fallen in love with my Land Rover. It was a sincere, deep-rooted response, as real as any other feeling of love. But it was yet another phantom emotion. I was lucky: I could recognise it for what it was, understand how it had come about and untangle myself from it. This was pretty much the last time I had any such struggle. My emotional checks and balances are back now and I hope not to fall head over heels with a rusty 4×4 again.

As each week went by after coming out of hospital, I looked back over it and realised how far I still had to go in recovery. I would sit and consider the things I found difficult and challenging in that week, things I would have breezed through before, and I have breathed a huge sigh of relief that I was better. And then another week would go by and I would look back over it in turn and realise once more that I was still in recovery, still had far to go. It is a long and sometimes tough process. The doctors, medics and nurses saved my life and gave me back my mind, but I then had to re-learn subtle lessons in how to use the fully functioning brain they had given back to me. It's still going on. I look back now on last week, think about the low points, the confusing moments and the difficult patches, and realise that even over a year after I started out I am still trudging along that road to recovery. And I thank every one of my lucky stars that I am able to make that trudge.

I did get out to the Arctic in the end. My skiing improved, though hardly to Olympic standards. I battled on through temperatures of minus forty, covering thirty or forty miles a day on foot and on skis. And yes, there were times when I also battled with demons inside that perhaps would not have been there before. But through every long, tough mile, I was overwhelmed with relief and a strange joy at being able to feel the pain, accept it and battle on. I had, by then, accepted that the damage to my brain would sometimes mean I struggled with things that were easier before, and it no longer scared me. It was no more frightening than feeling the occasional twinge from a once-broken arm.

I got back to the *Top Gear* studio too. The boys cooked up

a few gags for my return and we played it partly for laughs. But at the same time we knew we were dealing with something sensitive, not just for me and the team, but for anyone else affected in any way by the thousands of car crashes that happen every day. We did not want to make light of accidents and of brain injuries such as mine, but we could not gloss over the whole event and pretend to the world that in the fantastic TV world of *Top Gear* things don't go wrong. They do, they did, and we all learned lessons as a result. Most of all, perhaps, we learned that you owe it to yourself and those around you to look very carefully at what you are doing, to consider the risks and to take whatever measures you can to prepare for them. Standing once more on the *Top Gear* stage, I silently thanked every member of the team for ensuring through their diligence and professionalism that when I did something dangerous and difficult and was hit by disaster, I stood a chance of making it through.

This is not a sad or miserable story, not by a million miles. Yes, there are things I still have to work through even now, but I am here to work on them. The lessons I have learned, about myself and the world around me, have far outweighed the personal discomfort and occasional misery. I do feel for my family though. Mindy, my daughters, my parents and brothers had to stand and watch and worry when they were told I might die or be changed for ever. That is not a lesson to be embraced and enjoyed, that is just a very hard thing to have to do. Perhaps, though, by coming through it together, by weathering a considerable storm, we are closer and stronger than before.

Of course, there are thousands who are not so lucky. While visiting the Brain Injury Rehabilitation Centre in Bristol for check-ups and chats with Dr Holloway, I saw many other brain-injury victims working through their problems. People for whom the last memory before their world was turned upside down really was of riding a bike to the shops for a loaf of bread, or driving to work. The bravery, determination and sheer force of humanity of them, their doctors and nurses and their families watching on, is difficult to contemplate, but inspiring none-theless.

I've learned too that it can be tricky for people recovering from an injury to their brain, if only because often there is no visible external sign that anything is wrong. You cannot see that someone has damaged their memory, their emotions, their personality. They may look perfectly well on the outside but be suffering all manner of turmoil in their minds. I wanted at one point in my own recovery to wear a T-shirt that on one side read *I'm OK, please stop asking* but on the back read *I'm still bloody poorly, you know!* Both the best and the worst thing was when people looked at me, assumed I was fine and carried on as if nothing had ever happened. It was great to be able to forget about the accident and move on, but at the same time I needed people to understand the trouble I might still be having doing ordinary stuff. I think by now, though, I could lose the panel on the back and just have *I'm fine, thanks* printed on both sides.

The one thing that has never been a pain, though, is when people come up and ask how I am. They will often worry that perhaps I am tired of people asking, or resent the enquiry. Why would I? Who wouldn't want people asking about their health? Every time a pleasant middle-aged lady I have never met before walks up to me, puts her hand on my arm, looks into my eyes and asks how I am, it's as though an aunt has given me a big hug and asked the same question. It's comforting and healing, if only because it's a reminder that it's rather good to be a human being after all. So I will never be able to thank enough the people who wrote to me and thought about me when I was ill. It was a moving and powerful experience, and it contributed, I'm sure, to my recovery, and to Mindy's ability to cope with almost unthinkable pressure.

And so life gets ever closer to returning to what was normal for us. Of course, as our 'normal' includes days when I set out to try to reach the North Pole by dog sled, cross the English Channel in a floating van or even drive a jet car up an airfield in Yorkshire, we can never entirely relax. My driving licence came back in good time, largely because the surgeons had managed to avoid opening my skull. When it did, I grabbed the keys to my trusty Morgan and, with Mindy by my side, cruised round the country lanes near our home. The doctors had been worried about possible flashbacks and repercussions when first I drove. In fact, it never crossed my mind. What happened to me happened in a jet car. If I had fired up my Morgan and heard a jet engine start immediately behind my head, I might have had a bit of a moment. But this was different, this was just driving, and I loved it.

We laughed a lot. So did Izzy and Willow when I first took them for a drive a few days later.

'Daddy, are you driving?'

'Yes, I am, because the doctors said I can now.'

'Cool.'

They sat in silence and exaggerated concentration.

'Daddy?' they both asked together in their sing-song voices.

'Yes?'

'Don't go upside down and bang your head again, will you?

We'll all have to go to hospital then, and who will look after the horses?'

They laughed and laughed and laughed at their joke.

It's a routine we still go through every time we all get into Mindy's bright yellow Land Rover and set off on a family trip, even just to the shops. And in answer to their advice, I always say, 'No, no, I won't go on the roof again.' And if I can help it at all, I shan't.

Sitting beside me when I say that, as she has been through the highest and lowest points in my life, and the moments when it looked like it very well might end, is Mindy. The impact of any such accident is felt initially by the person at the front line, the one turned into a patient by it; but from that point on it becomes a burden to be carried by those closest to them. So I thank my parents, my brothers and my friends for being there when I needed them, and I am sorry for putting them through a tough time. My daughters were largely shielded from the hurt of it, but they missed their daddy, and one day I'll be able to explain why and say sorry to them too. And to Mindy I can only ever say a simple thank you. And dedicate the rest of my life to her.

ACKNOWLEDGEMENTS

This is the story of how I came to be prepared to risk losing my life, and very nearly did, and then, with the help of many, many people, got it back again. It is also the story of how an event such as my crash in September 2006 affected not just me, but those around me. Picking up the phone to be told that your husband, son or brother has crashed a jet-powered car and has sustained serious brain injuries is not an easy thing to do. I have many people to thank, therefore – those who put me back together again, physically, mentally and emotionally.

My thanks, first, to the Yorkshire Air Ambulance, and to the teams at Leeds and Bristol who were instrumental in my recovery and who kept Mindy sane and focused. At Leeds General Infirmary: John Adams, Consultant Neuro Anaesthetist; Sister Susan Aitchison; Elaine Andrews, Matron/Head of Nursing for Neurosciences; Michelle Ayling, Nursing Assistant; Andy Bennett, Charge Nurse, Neuro High Dependency Unit (HDU); Mark Brocksom, Head of Portering; Sara Costie, Staff Nurse, Neuro Intensive Care Unit (NICU); Fiona Evans, Sister, Neuro HDU; Nicola Fenton, Sister, NICU; Nicki Gibbs, Occupational Therapist; Jim Jackson, Senior Charge Nurse, NICU; Steve King, Senior Charge Nurse, NICU;

Charlie Lobley, Sister, Neurosurgery; Roberto Ramirez, Specialist Registrar, Neurosurgery; Stuart Ross, Consultant Neurosurgeon; Louise Rymer, Senior Sister, Neurosurgery; Kate Warner, Senior Physiotherapist; Karen Wilcock-Collins, Acquired Brain Injury Coordinator.

In A & E at Leeds General Infirmary: Shirley Wilson, Acting Matron, Accident & Emergency Services; day shift nurses Sister Laura Smith and Staff Nurse Cheryl Fenwick; night shift Charge Nurse Alan Sheward and Staff Nurse Asiscolo Prudenciado; Medical Staff Consultant Dr Peter Cutting; Specialist Registrar Dominic Hewitt; all the housekeeping and domestic staff on Ward 23, Neurosurgery; and the Patient Relations and Communications departments.

At The Glen BUPA Hospital in Bristol: Onyx Brewin, Sister; Michelle Osborne, Sister; Louise Daniel, Clinical Services Manager; Brin Rees-Evans, Head of Clinical Services; Sandie Foxall-Smith, General Manager; Jamie Noble, Physio Manager; Catherine Garrett, Senior Physiotherapist; Sarah Wring-Nash, Hotel Services Coordinator; Alan Sheppard, Chief Engineer; Rick Nelson, Consultant Neurosurgeon; Pat Easterbrook, Sister; Andrew Martin, Reception Manager.

And at the Frenchay Centre for Brain Injury Rehabilitation, Bristol: Dr John Holloway and his team.

Mum, Mum and Dad, Andy and Andrea, Nick and Amanda. All friends and neighbours, especially Anne and Syd, Beano and Michelle, Pat and Steve, Fiona and Malcolm, Colin Goodwin, Andy Hodgson, Ela Turz, Jenni Schmit, Katrina Tanzer, Zog and Jill Ziegler and Bill Scott. Gary Farrow. The *Top Gear* team, especially Andy Wilman, Alex Renton and Grant Wardrop. Professor Syd Watkins, Arai Helmets, Racelogic, the Operation

Joystick team and all the people who looked after us in the Scottish Highlands.

And to my entire family: sorry, won't do it again.